LifeThemes

S E R I E S

Great Grace

A 31-Day Devotional

⤳

J.I. PACKER
COMPILED BY BETH FEIA

VINE
BOOKS

SERVANT PUBLICATIONS
ANN ARBOR, MICHIGAN

Scripture used in the work, unless otherwise indicated, is taken from the HOLY
BIBLE: NEW INTERNATIONAL VERSION® (NIV®) © 1973, 1978, 1984
International Bible Society. Used by permission of Zondervan Bible Publishers.
Excerpts from *Concise Theology: A Guide to Historic Christian Beliefs* © 1993 by
Foundation for Reformation. Used by permission of Tyndale House Publishers, Inc.
All rights reserved. Excerpts from *Hot Tub Religion* © 1987 by J.I. Packer. Used by
permission of Tyndale House Publishers, Inc. All rights reserved. Excerpts from
God's Words © 1988 by J.I. Packer. Used by permission of Baker Book House
Company. Excerpts from *Knowing God* © 1973 by J.I. Packer. Used by permission
of InterVarsity Press, P.O. Box 1400, Downers Grove, IL 60515. All rights reserved.
Excerpts from *Our Savior God* © 1980 by James M. Borce. Used by permission of
Baker Book House Company.

Vine Books is an imprint of Servant Publications especially designed to serve evangel-
ical Christians.

Published by Servant Publications
P.O. Box 8617
Ann Arbor, Michigan 48107

Cover photo: © M. Neveux/Westlight. Used by permission.
Cover design: Diane Bareis

97 98 99 00 01 10 9 8 7 6 5 4 3 2 1

Printed in the United States of America
ISBN 1-56955-031-X

LIBRARY OF CONGRESS CATALOGING-IN-PUBLICATION DATA

Packer, J.I. (James Innell)
Great grace : a 31-day devotional / J.I. Packer ; compiled by Beth Feia.
    p.   cm.
Includes bibliographical references.
ISBN 1-56955-031-X
1. Grace.   2. Devotional calendars.   I. Feia, Beth.   II. Title.
BT761.2.P33   1997
234—dc21

                                                          97-9035
                                                          CIP

Contents

To the Reader / 7

Amazing Grace
1. The Wonder of Grace/13
2. Who God Is and Who You Are/17
3. Let Grace Sweep You Off Your Feet/23

The Master's Plan
4. History Is God's Story/29
5. God's Glorious Plan/33
6. God Wants Us to Be Holy/37
7. Divine Teamwork/41

Redeeming Love in Action
8. God's Justice in His Mercy/45
9. His Suffering Love/49
10. His Giving Love/53
11. His Saving Love/57
12. The Power of His Spirit/61

The Aspects of Grace
13. The Great Rescue/67
14. Chosen, Called, Saved, and Kept/71
15. Christ Paid the Debt That You Could Never Pay/75
16. Growing in Family Likeness/79
17. Desiring God and His Holiness/83

Growth in Grace

18. Growing Up in Christ/89
19. Living Out What God Has Done/93
20. Signs of Growth/97
21. Being Remade/101
22. The Means of Growth/105

Trouble on the Road to Glory

23. Pain: God's Chisel for Sculpting Our Souls /111
24. In God's Hospital/115
25. Three Mistakes to Avoid/119
26. Glorify God in Your Suffering/123

Saying Yes to New Life

27. Consecrating Yourself to God/129
28. Living a Life Worthy/133
29. How Can I Repay the Lord?/137
30. Just Say "No" to Sin/141
31. Nothing Can Dash You from His Hand/145

Bibliography / 147

To the Reader

꒰

When I was young, I heard Jack Benny perform in a radio show the following bit of crosstalk.

BANDIT: Your money or your life!
COMEDIAN (after a long, long pause): I'm thinking it over.

"Thinking it over" is the activity which in its Christian form is called meditation.

Christian meditation—not to be confused with its Hindu, Buddhist, or New Age counterpart—is thinking over in God's presence what God tells or shows us about himself and ourselves. It is an exercise of realization and application, leading on to direct address to God in the speech and song of prayer and praise. It is a preparatory talking to ourselves, focusing upon things about which we must now talk to God. It is a habit of the Christian life that monastics practiced from the start and that Protestants and Catholics have long urged that all should learn; nowadays, however, it is widely neglected. Materials for meditation are provided here in hope of helping Christians to rediscover this lost art. My local paper advertises cut-price trial periods at fitness centers, where planned physical exercises make bodies slim, supple, and strong; clearly the hope is that the good effects of the trial period will hook you in (at full rates, of course) for the rest of your days. What is offered here is devotional meditations for a month, and my hope is that, whether or not you were a meditator before, the month's experience will make this happy and fruitful activity a regular part of your life with God.

What should Christians be thinking over as they talk to themselves in preparation for talking to God? In general, the biblical revelation of God in Creation, Providence, and grace, and one's own life as Scripture assesses it; in particular, biblical truths about the Lord Jesus Christ, and the love and wisdom of Jesus as displayed in the Gospel stories. Meditation on these things clears the head and makes the heart warm and honest as we approach God. It would be uncouth to compare meditation with manure, but it is a fact that faith, hope, and love, along with zeal and joy, grow stronger in meditative souls than elsewhere.

How should this book be used? Not as an alternative to reading the Bible itself, *please;* that would be like trying to live on butter or jam without bread! My hope is that you will take its sections in order, one a day, and that when you have digested each piece of Packer, looking up the texts, thinking through the thoughts, and asking what there is here to prompt praise and petition, you will move to the hymn, and use it as your verbal vehicle for both.

The hymns chosen are in prayer or pre-prayer form already, and if you are anything like me you will be much enriched by first elaborating and then re-concentrating their line of thought (just as you would when praying the Lord's Prayer or a psalm), and so making them the expression of your own heart. Turning hymns into personal prayers is a help and a delight that too few Christians nowadays know about.

Then I hope you will move on from *Great Grace* (the book—not the theme!) and continue your fellowship time with God just as you find yourself wanting to do. This book is offered you as a spur and a starter, like the appetizer at a banquet; you advance from it to the rest of the meal.

Since all the studies deal with aspects of gospel grace, which is the true starting-point for Christian devotion, some repetition is unavoidable, and I think healthy, and I do not apologize for it. Beth Feia selected the materials most skillfully, and I wish to record here my thanks to her for her labors.

J.I. Packer

Amazing Grace

-1-
The Wonder of Grace

In the New Testament, "grace" is a word of central importance—the keyword, in fact, of Christianity. Grace is what the New Testament is about. Its God is "the God of all grace" (1 Peter 5:10); its Holy Spirit is "the Spirit of grace" (Hebrews 10:29); and all the hopes that it sets forth rest upon "the grace of our Lord Jesus" (Acts 15:11), the Lord who upheld Paul with the assurance, "my grace is sufficient for you" (2 Corinthians 12:9). "Grace," says John, "came through Jesus Christ" (John 1:17); and the news about Jesus is accordingly "the gospel of God's grace" (Acts 20:24).

The apostles' belief in the reality and centrality of grace was so strong that it led them to invent a new style of letter-writing. Instead of the conventional "hail," the opening greeting of thirteen of Paul's letters takes the form of a prayer for "grace and peace," or "grace, mercy, and peace," from God the Father and the Lord Jesus Christ, to be upon his readers; and in place of the usual "farewell," each letter ends with a further prayer that "the grace of the Lord Jesus Christ," or "grace" simply, may be with them. And everything that comes between the salutation and the benediction of these letters illustrates the truth that grace was to the apostles the fundamental fact of Christian life.

It is often said, and truly, that the theme of the New Testament is salvation. But the New Testament salvation is of grace from first to last (see Ephesians 2:5,8); it is the grace of God that brings it (see Titus 2:11), and the praise of the glory of God's grace that is the end of it (see Ephesians 1:6). It thus appears that, rightly understood, this one word "grace" contains within itself the whole of New Testament theology. The New Testament message is just the announcement that grace has come to us in and through Jesus Christ, plus a summons from God to receive this grace (see Romans 5:17; 2 Corinthians 6:1), and to know it (see Colossians 1:6), and not to frustrate it (see Galatians 2:21), but to continue in it (see Acts 13:43), since "the word of his grace... which can build you up, and give you an inheritance among all those who are sanctified" (Acts 20:32). Grace is the sum and substance of New Testament faith.

Grace is God's undeserved favor, his unmerited love. The word "grace" expresses the thought of God acting in spontaneous goodness to save sinners: God loving the unlovely, making covenant with them, pardoning their sins, accepting their persons, revealing himself to them, moving them to response, leading them ultimately into full knowledge and enjoyment of himself, and overcoming all obstacles to the fulfillment of this purpose that at each stage arise. Grace is election-love plus covenant-love, a free choice issuing in a sovereign work. Grace saves from sin and all evil; grace brings ungodly humans to true happiness in the knowledge of their Maker. This is the concept of grace with which the New Testament writers work.

> *[The New Testament writers] find it simply staggering that there should be such a thing as grace at all—let alone grace that was so costly to God as the grace of Calvary.*

To the New Testament writers, grace is a wonder. Their sense of man's corruption and demerit before God, and of the reality and justice of his wrath against sin, is so strong that they find it simply staggering that there should be such a thing as grace at all—let alone grace that was so costly to God as the grace of Calvary. The hymn-writers catch this sense of wonder with their use of "amazed" and "amazing" in such lines as "*Amazing* love! How can it be/ That thou, my God, shouldst die for me?"; "Love so amazing, so divine,/ Demands my soul, my life, my all"; "I stand all amazed at the love Jesus offers me"; "*Amazing* grace!" The world is full of wonders—wonders of nature, wonders of science, wonders of craftsmanship—but they pale into insignificance beside the wonder of the grace of God. Nothing we say can do it justice: all words fall short of it: it is in truth, as Paul says, an "inexpressible gift" (2 Corinthians 9:15).

God's Words, pp. 94-99

ॐ

Amazing grace! How sweet the sound
That saved a wretch like me!
I once was lost but now am found,
Was blind but now I see.

'Twas grace that taught my heart to fear,
And grace my fears relieved;
How precious did that grace appear
The hour I first believed!

Through many dangers, toils, and snares,
I have already come;
'Tis grace hath brought me safe thus far,
And grace will lead me home.

-2-

Who God Is and Who You Are

Many church people pay lip service to the idea of grace, but there they stop. Their conception of grace is not so much debased as nonexistent. The thought means nothing to them; it does not touch their experience at all.

Faith in grace is a rarity today.

What is it that hinders so many who profess to believe in grace from really doing so? Why does the theme mean so little even to some who talk about it a great deal? The root of the trouble seems to be misbelief about the basic relationship between a person and God—misbelief rooted not just in the mind but in the heart, at the deeper level of things that we never question because we always take them for granted. There are four critical truths in this realm which the doctrine of grace presupposes, and if they are not acknowledged and felt in one's heart, clear faith in God's grace becomes impossible. Unhappily, the spirit of our age is as directly opposed to them as it well could be. It is not to be wondered at, therefore, that faith in grace is a rarity today. The four truths are these:

1. The moral ill-desert of humankind. Modern men and women, conscious of the tremendous scientific and technological achievements in recent years, naturally incline to a high opinion of themselves. They view material wealth as more important than moral character, and in the moral realm they are resolutely kind to themselves, treating small virtues as compensating for great vices and refusing to take seriously the idea that, morally speaking, there is anything much wrong with them.

For modern men and women are convinced that, despite all their little peccadilloes—drinking, gambling, reckless driving, sexual laxity, black and white lies, sharp practices in trading, dirty reading, and what have you—they are at heart thoroughly good folks. Then, as pagans do (and the hearts of modern people are pagan—make no mistake about that), they imagine God as a magnified image of themselves, and assume that God shares their own complacency about themselves. The thought of themselves as creatures fallen from God's image, rebels against God's rule, guilty and unclean in God's sight, fit only for God's condemnation, never enters their heads.

2. The retributive justice of God. The way of modern men and women is to turn a blind eye to all wrongdoing as long as they safely can. They tolerate it in others, feeling that there, but for the accident of circumstances, go they themselves. Willingness to tolerate and indulge evil up to the limit is seen as a virtue, while living by fixed principles of right and wrong is censured by some as doubtfully moral.

In our pagan way, we take it for granted that God feels as we do. The idea that retribution might be the moral law of God's world and an expression of his holy character seems to us quite fantastic. Yet the Bible insists throughout that this world which God in his goodness has made is a moral world, one in which retribution is as basic a fact as breathing.

3. The spiritual impotence of humankind. Dale Carnegie's *How to Win Friends and Influence People* has been almost a modern Bible. In recent years a whole technique of business relations has been built on the principle of putting the other person in a position where he cannot decently say no. This has confirmed modern men and women in the faith that has animated pagan religion ever since there was such a thing—namely, the belief that we can repair our own relationship with God by putting God in a position where he cannot say no to us anymore.

Ancient pagans thought to do this by multiplying gifts and sacrifices; modern pagans seek to do it by church membership and morality. Conceding that we are not perfect, we still have no doubt that respectability henceforth will guarantee God's acceptance of us in the end, whatever we may have done in the past.

4. The sovereign freedom of God. Ancient paganism thought of each god as bound to his worshipers by bonds of self-interest, because he depended on their service and gifts for his welfare. Modern paganism has at the back of its mind a similar feeling that God is somehow obliged to love and help us, little though we deserve it. This was the feeling voiced by the French freethinker who died muttering, "God will forgive—that's his job *(c'est son métier)*." But this feeling is not well founded. The God of the Bible does not depend on his human creatures for his well-being (see Psalm 50:8-13; Acts 17:25), nor, now that we have sinned, is he bound to show us favor.

We can only claim from him justice—and justice, for us, means certain condemnation. God does not owe it to anyone to stop justice from taking its course. He is not obliged to pity and pardon; if he does so it is an act done, as we say, "of his own free will," and nobody forces his hand. "It does not...depend on man's desire or effort, but on God's mercy" (Romans 9:16). Grace is free, in the sense of being self-originated and of proceeding from One who was not obliged to be gracious. Only when it is seen that what decides each individual's destiny is whether or not God resolves to save him from his sins, and that this is a decision which God need not make in any single case, can one begin to grasp the biblical view of grace.

Knowing God, pp. 129-32

Alas! And did my Savior bleed
And did my sovereign die?
Would He devote that sacred Head
For such a worm as I?

Was it for crimes that I had done,
He groaned upon the tree?
Amazing pity, grace unknown!
And love beyond degree!

Well might the sun in darkness hide,
And shut His glories in;
When God, the mighty Maker, died,
For man the creature's sin.

Thus might I hide my blushing face,
While Jesus' Cross appears;
Dissolve my heart in thankfulness,
And melt my eyes in tears.

But drops of grief can ne'er repay
The debt of love I owe;
Here, Lord, I give myself away;
'Tis all that I can do.

-3-

Let Grace Sweep You Off Your Feet

The grace of God is love freely shown toward guilty sinners, contrary to their merit and indeed in defiance of their demerit. It is God showing goodness to persons who deserve only severity and had no reason to expect anything but severity. We have seen why the thought of grace means so little to some church people— namely, because they do not share the beliefs about God and man which it presupposes. Now we have to ask, why should this thought mean so much to others? It is surely clear that, once people are convinced that their state and need are as described, the New Testament gospel of grace cannot but sweep them off their feet with wonder and joy. For it tells how our Judge has become our Savior.

Our Judge has become our Savior.

Grace and salvation belong together as cause and effect. "It is by grace you have been saved" (Ephesians 2:5, 8). "The grace of God that brings salvation has appeared" (Titus 2:11). The gospel declares how "God so loved the world that he gave his one and only Son, that whoever believes in him shall not perish but have eternal life" (John 3:16); how "God demonstrates his own love for us in this: While we were still sinners, Christ died for us" (Romans 5:8); how a fountain has been opened, according to

23

prophecy (see Zechariah 13:1), for sin and for uncleanness.

The New Testament sets forth the grace of God in three particular connections, each of them a perpetual marvel to the Christian believer.

1. Grace as the source of the pardon of sin. The gospel centers upon justification—that is, upon the remission of sins and the acceptance of our persons that goes with it. Justification is the truly dramatic transition from the status of a condemned criminal awaiting a terrible sentence to that of an heir awaiting a fabulous inheritance.

Justification is by faith; it takes place the moment a person puts vital trust in the Lord Jesus Christ as Savior. Justification is free to us, but it was costly to God, for its price was the atoning death of God's Son. Why was it that God "did not spare his own Son, but gave him up for us all" (Romans 8:32)? Because of his grace. It was his own free decision to save which brought about the atonement. Paul makes this explicit. We are justified, he says, "freely" [with nothing to pay] by his grace [in consequence of God's merciful resolve] through the redemption that came by Christ Jesus.

2. Grace as the motive of the plan of salvation. Pardon is the heart of the gospel, but it is not the whole doctrine of grace. For the New Testament sets God's gift of pardon in the context of a plan of salvation which began with election before the world was and will be completed only when the church is perfect in glory.

Paul refers briefly to this plan in several places (see, for instance, Romans 8:29-30; 2 Thessalonians 2:12-13). But his fullest account of it is in the massive paragraph—for, despite subdivisions, the flow of thought constitutes essentially one paragraph—running from Ephesians 1:3 to 2:10. As often, Paul starts with a summary statement and spends the rest of the paragraph analyzing and explaining it. The statement is, "God... has blessed us in the heavenly realms with every spiritual blessing in Christ" (v. 3).

The analysis begins with eternal election and predestination to sonship in Christ (vv. 4-5), proceeds to redemption and remission of sins in Christ (v. 7), and moves on to the hope of glorification in Christ (vv. 11-12) and the gift of the Spirit in Christ to seal us as God's possession forever (vv. 13-14).

From there, Paul concentrates attention on the act of power whereby God regenerates sinners in Christ (1:19; 2:7), bringing them to faith in the process (2:8). Paul depicts all these items as elements in a single great saving purpose (1:5, 9, 11), and tells us that grace (mercy, love, kindness: 2:4, 7) is its motivating force (see 2:4-8); that "the riches of God's grace" appear throughout its administration (1:7; 2:7); and that the praise of grace is its ultimate goal (1:6, compare 1:12, 14; 2:7). So we believers may rejoice to know that our conversion was no accident, but an act of God which had its place in an eternal plan to bless us with the free gift of salvation from sin (2:8-10); God promises and purposes to carry his plan through to completion, and since it is executed by sovereign power (1:19-20), nothing can thwart it. The stars, indeed, may fall, but God's promises will stand and be fulfilled. The plan of salvation will be brought to a triumphant completion; thus grace will be shown to be sovereign.

3. Grace as the guarantee of the preservation of the saints. If the plan of salvation is certain of accomplishment, then the Christian's future is assured. I am, and will be, "kept by the power of God through faith unto salvation" (1 Peter 1:5 KJV). I need not torment myself with the fear that my faith may fail; as grace led me to faith in the first place, so grace will keep me believing to the end. Faith, both in its origin and continuance, is a gift of grace (see Philippians 1:29).

Knowing God, pp. 132-36

But there's a voice of princely grace
Sounds from God's holy Word;
Ho! ye poor captive sinners, come,
And trust upon the Lord.

My soul obeys the sovereign call,
And runs to this relief;
I would believe thy promise, Lord,
Oh, help my unbelief.

To the blest fountain of thy blood,
Incarnate God, I fly,
To wash my soul from scarlet stains,
And sins of deepest dye.

A guilty, weak, and helpless worm,
Into thy hands I fall;
Thou art the Lord, my righteousness,
My Savior, and my all.

The Master's Plan

-4-
History Is God's Story

What do we find when we read the Bible as a single unified whole, with our minds alert to observe its real focus?

We find just this: This Bible is not primarily about humankind at all. Its subject is God. He (if the phrase may be allowed) is the chief actor in the drama, the hero of the story. The Bible is a factual survey of his work in this world, past, present, and future, with explanatory comments from prophets, psalmists, wise men, and apostles. Its main theme is not human salvation, but the work of God vindicating his purposes and glorifying himself in a sinful and disordered cosmos. He does this by establishing his kingdom and exalting his Son, by creating a people to worship and serve him, and ultimately by dismantling and reassembling this order of things, thereby rooting sin out of his world. It is into this larger perspective that the Bible fits God's work of saving mankind.

Though hostile forces rage and chaos threatens,
God is King; therefore his people are safe.

Scripture depicts God as more than a distant impersonal life-force. God is more than any of the petty substitute deities that inhabit our twentieth-century minds. He is the living God, present and active everywhere, "majestic in holiness, awesome in glory, working wonders" (Exodus 15:11). He gives himself a name—Yahweh (Jehovah: see Exodus 3:14-15; 6:2-3), which, whether it be translated "I am that I am" or "I will be that I will be" (the Hebrew means both), is a proclamation of his self-existence and self-sufficiency, his omnipotence and his unbounded freedom. This world is his, he made it, and he controls it. He "works out everything in conformity with the purpose of his will" (Ephesians 1:11). His knowledge and dominion extend to the smallest things: "The very hairs of your head are all numbered" (Matthew 10:30). "The Lord reigns"—the psalmists make this unchangeable truth the starting point for their praises again and again (see Psalms 93:1; 96:10; 97:1; 99:1).

Though hostile forces rage and chaos threatens, God is King; therefore his people are safe. Such is the God of the Bible. And the Bible's dominant conviction about him, a conviction proclaimed from Genesis to Revelation, is that behind and beneath all the apparent confusion of this world lies his plan. That plan concerned the perfecting of a people and the restoring of a world through the mediating action of Christ. God governs human affairs with this end in view. Human history is a record of the outworking of his purposes. History is his story.

Hot Tub Religion, pp. 13-15

Love divine, all loves excelling,
Joy of heaven to earth come down.
Fix in us Thy humble dwelling,
All Thy faithful mercies crown.
Jesus, Thou art all compassion,
Pure, unbounded love Thou art;
Visit us with Thy salvation,
Enter every trembling heart.

Breathe, O breathe Thy loving Spirit
Into every troubled breast!
Let us all in Thee inherit,
Let us find the promised rest!
Take away our bent to sinning;
Alpha and Omega be;
End of faith, as its beginning,
Set our hearts at liberty.

Come, Almighty to deliver,
Let us all Thy grace receive;
Suddenly return, and never,
Nevermore Thy temples leave.
Thee we would be always blessing,
Serve Thee as Thy hosts above,
Pray, and praise Thee without ceasing,
Glory in Thy perfect love.

Finish, then, Thy new creation;
Pure and spotless let us be;
Let us see Thy great salvation
Perfectly restored in Thee:
Changed from glory into glory,
Till in heaven we take our place,
Till we cast our crowns before Thee,
Lost in wonder, love, and praise.

-5-
God's Glorious Plan

The plan of salvation, which tells me how my Creator has become my Redeemer, sets before me in fullest glory the transcendent majesty that the churches have so largely forgotten. It shows me a God who is infinitely great in wisdom and power—who knew from all eternity what fallen humanity's plight would be—and who before creating the cosmos had already schemed out in detail how he would save not only me, but each single one of the many billions whom he was resolved to bring to glory. The plan tells me of a vast program for world history, a program involving millennia of providential preparation for the first coming of a Savior, and millennia more of worldwide evangelism, pastoral care, Christianizing of culture, demonstration of God's kingdom, spiritual warfare against its enemies, and building up of the church, before the Savior returns.

Just as there could be for Jesus no crown without the cross, so there can be for us no holiness without the praise.

The plan sets before me the Father sending the Son to redeem, and the Spirit to quicken, the lost and guilty living dead—dead souls like mine, dead in transgressions and sins, led by the devices and desires of a corrupt heart, and often putting up a smoke screen of religious formalism to keep the light of God from reaching my conscience. The plan covers not only (1) the three-hour

33

agony of Jesus on the cross, vicariously enduring Godforsakenness so that sinners like me would never have to endure it; but also (2) the permanently transforming bodily resurrection of Jesus and the permanently transforming heart-regeneration of everyone who is saved—two demonstrations of the power that made the world that are, be it said, wholly inexplicable in terms of the created forces that operate in the world. (Here then, is where apologetics should start.) Finally, the plan reaches into the future, promising everyone a new, undying body. In addition, it promises saved sinners like me a new heaven and earth, a vast perfected society, and the visible presence of Jesus, to enjoy through that new body forever.

Such are the wonders of the plan of salvation. God's call to holiness begins by telling me to dwell on these great and awesome realities until I find myself truly awestruck at the greatness of my God, who is making it all happen. In this way I will learn to give him glory (in the sense of praise) for the greatness of his glory (in the sense of self-display) as the One whose revealed wisdom and power, in redemption as in creation, dazzle, surpass, and overwhelm my understanding. The triune God of the plan is great—transcendent and immutable in his omnipotence, omniscience, and omnipresence. He is eternal in his truthfulness and faithfulness, wisdom and justice, severity and goodness—and he must be praised and adored as such. Praise of this kind is the doxological foundation of human holiness, which always starts here. Just as there could be for Jesus no crown without the cross, so there can be for us no holiness without the praise.

Rediscovering Holiness, pp. 69-70

Praise my soul, the King of heaven,
To His feet your tribute bring;
Ransomed, healed, restored, forgiven,
Who, like me, His praise should sing?
Alleluia! Alleluia! Praise the everlasting King!

Praise Him for His grace and favor
To our fathers in distress;
Praise Him, still the same forever,
Slow to chide and swift to bless.
Praise Him! Praise Him! Praise Him! Praise Him!
Glorious in His faithfulness.

Fatherlike, He tends and spares us,
Well our feeble frame He knows;
In His hands He gently bears us,
Rescues us from all our foes;
Alleluia! Alleluia! Widely as His mercy flows!

Angels help us to adore Him,
You behold Him face to face;
Sun and moon, bow down before Him;
Dwellers all in time and space,
Alleluia! Alleluia! Praise with us the God of grace!

-6-

God Wants Us to Be Holy

God is saving a great company of sinners. He has been engaged in this task since history began. He spent many centuries preparing a people and a setting of world history for the coming of his Son. Then he sent his Son into the world in order that there might be a gospel, and now he sends his gospel throughout the world in order that there may be a church. He has exalted his Son to the throne of the universe, and Christ from his throne now invites sinners to himself. He keeps them, leads them, and finally brings them to be with him in his glory.

God is saving men and women through his Son. First he justifies and adopts them into his family for Christ's sake as soon as they believe and thus restores the relationship between them and himself that sin had broken. Then within that restored relationship, God continually works in and upon them to renew them in the image of Christ, so that the family likeness (if the phrase may be allowed) shall appear in them more and more. It is this renewal of ourselves, progressive here and to be perfected hereafter, that Paul identifies with the "good" when he writes, "in all things God works for the good of those who love him, who have been called according to his purpose" (Romans 8:28). God's purpose, as Paul explains, is that those whom God has chosen and in love has called to himself should "be conformed to the likeness of his Son, that he [the Son] might be the firstborn among many brothers" (Romans 8:29). All God's ordering of circumstances, Paul tells us, is designed for the fulfillment of this purpose. The "good" for which all things work is not the immediate ease and comfort of

God's children (as is, one fears, too often supposed), but their ultimate holiness and conformity to the likeness of Christ.

God's purpose is that those whom God has chosen and in love has called to himself should be conformed to the likeness of his Son.

Does this help us to understand how adverse circumstances may find a place in God's plan for his people? Certainly! It throws a flood of light upon the problem, as the writer of the Letter to the Hebrews demonstrates. To Christians who had grown disheartened and apathetic under the pressure of constant hardship and victimization, we find him writing: "Have you forgotten the exhortation which addresses you as sons?—'My son, do not regard lightly the discipline of the Lord, nor lose courage when you are punished [better, reproved, KJV] by him. For the Lord disciplines him whom he loves, and chastises every son whom he receives.' It is for discipline that you have to endure. God is treating you as sons; for what son is there whom his father does not discipline? ... We have had earthly fathers to discipline us and we respected them. Shall we not much more be subject to the Father of spirits and live? ... He disciplines us *for our good, that we may share his holiness.* For the moment all discipline seems painful rather than pleasant; later it yields the peaceful fruit of righteousness to those who have been trained by it" (Hebrews 12:5-11, RSV, quoting Proverbs 3:11-12, emphasis added). It is striking to see how this writer, like Paul, equates the Christian's "good," not with ease and quiet, but with sanctification. The passage is so plain that it needs no comment, only frequent rereading whenever we find it hard to believe that the rough handling that circumstances (or our fellow Christians) are giving us can possibly be God's will.

Hot Tub Religion, pp. 22-24

The King of love my Shepherd is,
Whose goodness faileth never;
I nothing lack if I am His
And He is mine forever.

Perverse and foolish oft I strayed,
But yet in love He sought me,
And on His shoulder gently laid,
And home rejoicing brought me.

In death's dark vale I fear no ill
With Thee, dear Lord, beside me;
Thy rod and staff my comfort still,
Thy cross before to guide me.

And so, through all the length of days
Thy goodness faileth never
Good Shepherd may I sing Thy praise
Within Thy house forever.

-7-
Divine Teamwork

New Testament salvation is the joint work of a divine trio, a team consisting of the Father, Son, and Holy Spirit. It is, indeed, in the process of expounding the cooperative saving action of the holy Three that the New Testament brings out their personal distinctness within the unity of God. The truth of the Trinity thus emerges as part of the doctrine of salvation. Their roles are set forth as follows.

The Father, who planned everything (Romans 8:28-30; Ephesians 3:9-11), sent first the Son and then the Spirit into the world to carry out his saving intentions (John 3:17; 6:38-40; 14:26; 16:7-15; Romans 8:26).

The Son, whose nature and joy it is to always do the Father's will (John 4:34; 5:19; 6:38; 8:29), became man in order to die for us, rise for us, reign for us, and one day return for us to take us to the place of happy rest that he has prepared for us (John 10:14-18; 14:2; 18-23). In the meantime, he mediates mercy and help to us from his throne (Hebrews 4:14-16; 7:25).

Just as mutual love and honor is revealed as the occupation of the Three-in-One, so loving and honoring the Trinity becomes the eternal vocation of those whom the Three-in-One have saved— starting now!

The Holy Spirit, the self-effacing divine executive who engineered creation (Genesis 1:2) and now engineers the new creation (John 3:3-8), has been at work since Pentecost imparting to believers their first installment of heaven's life in and with their Savior (Romans 8:23; Ephesians 1:13). In addition, the Holy Spirit is changing believers progressively into Christ's image (2 Corinthians 3:18).

Salvation is thus the threefold activity of the triune God. Just as mutual love and honor are revealed as the occupation of the Three-in-One (John 3:35; 5:20; 14:31; 16:14; 17:1,4), so loving and honoring the Trinity becomes the eternal vocation of those whom the Three-in-One have saved—starting now! One mark of the saved, therefore, is that they currently give themselves to worship, and they want to go on doing so literally forever.

Rediscovering Holiness, pp. 48-49

Father most holy, merciful and loving,
Jesus, Redeemer, ever to be worshipped,
Life-giving Spirit, Comforter most gracious,
God everlasting!

Three in a wondrous Unity unbroken,
One perfect Godhead, love that never faileth,
Light of the angels, succor of the needy.
Hope of all living.

Lord God Almighty, unto Thee be glory,
One in three Persons, over all exalted,
Thine, as is meet, be honor, praise and blessing
Now and forever!

Redeeming Love
in Action

❧

-8-

God's Justice in His Mercy

Righteousness is that quality in God whereby he always does what is right, the quality whereby he maintains and meets the claims of the past in the present, giving to every person his or her due. That was Aristotle's definition of human righteousness, and it is the fundamental biblical view of the righteousness of God also. God gives us what is due to us.

This makes the righteousness of God in judgment very easy to understand, but it makes the righteousness of God in justifying the sinner appear at first inexplicable because it sounds wrong. It is marvelous good news. But surely, we say, it is not right that God, the just judge, should justify the ungodly, as Paul in Romans 4:5 says he actually does. Can it be right for God to behave this way? That is the question to which Paul is addressing himself in the compressed words of Romans 3:25-26. And he is telling us here that it really is right. It has become right. It has become the only right thing for God to do in virtue of his having sent his Son to be our sin-bearer.

This aspect of righteousness, whereby claims are met, was described in Roman law as "satisfaction" *(satisfactio)*, which means "doing enough *(satis facere)* to meet the claims that are there." Paul is saying that God justifies us in a way that fully meets the claims that are there. So since the time of the great Anselm, the Christian church has rejoiced to use this word satisfaction as a term expressing the real significance of the sacrifice of Christ. As Anselm expounded satisfaction, it was a matter of satisfying God's

45

outraged honor, and that indeed is part of the truth. But when Luther came along, he broadened the idea of satisfaction to what he found in the Bible, and he made the right and true point that the satisfaction of Jesus Christ restores God's glory through Christ's enduring full penal retribution for our sin. The satisfaction of Christ glorifies God the Father and wins salvation for the sinner by being a satisfaction to God's justice. That is the thought Paul is expressing in Romans 3:25-26.

Since the time of the great Anselm, the Christian church has rejoiced to use this word satisfaction as a term expressing the real significance of the sacrifice of Christ.

Paul tells us that God set forth his Son to be a propitiation by his blood. This, says Paul, was "to demonstrate his justice, because in his forbearance he had left the sins committed beforehand unpunished." He had indeed justified sinners. He had been doing it throughout the whole Old Testament period. But he had been doing it on no more substantial a basis than the offering of animal sacrifice. Anyone who thought about things might well have raised the question, "How can the death of an animal put away the sin of a man?" There was no answer to that question once it was raised. So right up to the death of the Lord Jesus a great question mark hung over God's grace in forgiving sins. Men praised God for the mercy, but they could not see its basis in righteousness. But now you can see it, says Paul. Now it is made plain. The redemption that is in Christ Jesus removes the question mark. God's redeeming action had retrospective efficacy; but not only that, it has efficacy in the present and for the future also. For Paul goes on to say, "He did it to demonstrate his justice at the present time, so as to be just and the one who justifies the man who has faith in Jesus" (v. 26).

46

In other words, through the redemption that is in Christ Jesus justice is done. On the cross, sin is punished as it deserves. But it is punished in the person of a substitute. Now we can see how it is that God's justification is just. Now we can see how God's justification of sinners is itself justified. God has shown his righteousness. He has satisfied himself, rendering the satisfaction that was due his own holiness. And so men may go free. God propitiated himself, we may say. God both gave and received satisfaction through the death of his Son, Jesus Christ.

That is why the word satisfaction has become a precious word to the people of God down the centuries—as, for instance, in the prescribed communion service in the historic prayer book of the Anglican church: "Almighty God, our heavenly Father, who of thy tender mercy didst give thine only Son Jesus Christ to die upon the cross for our salvation, who made there, by his one oblation of himself once offered, a full, perfect and sufficient sacrifice, oblation and satisfaction for the sins of the whole world...." Or as in the Heidelberg Catechism: "My only comfort in life and death is that I belong to my faithful Savior Jesus Christ, who with his precious blood has fully satisfied for all my sins."

"Sacrifice and Satisfaction," pp. 125-29

We come, O Christ, to Thee, True Son of God and man,
By Whom all things consist, in Whom all life began:
In Thee alone we live and move,
And have our being in Thy love.

Thou art the Way to God, Thy blood our ransom paid;
In Thee we face our Judge and Maker unafraid.
Before the throne absolved we stand:
Thy love has met Thy law's demand.

-9-
His Suffering Love

The cross of Christ is a revelation of the love of God, for it reveals what that love is prepared to suffer for the one loved. I believe that the presentation of the death of Christ as substitution exhibits the love of the cross more richly, fully, gloriously, and glowingly than does any other presentation. It gets us nearer to the heart of that love than any of the other pictures that the New Testament contains.

Luther saw it and gloried in the fact that the man who knows Christ can be assured of such love. He once wrote to a friend, "Learn to know Christ and him crucified. Learn to pray to him, and despairing of yourself to say this, 'Lord Jesus, you are my righteousness, I am your sin. You have taken upon yourself what is mine and given me what is yours. You have made me what I was not, by taking to yourself what you were not.'" There has been an exchange, a great and wonderful exchange. Luther actually used that phrase, a "wonderful exchange." He knew that the Son of God has taken upon himself all our guilt and set upon us all his righteousness. Was there ever such love?

> *The cross of Christ is a revelation of the love of God, for it reveals what that love is prepared to suffer for the one loved.*

Rabbi Duncan was a great Reformed teacher in New College, Edinburgh, a little over a hundred years ago. In one of his famous excursions in his classes, where he would move off from the

Hebrew he was supposed to be teaching to theological reflections on this or that, he threw out the following question: "Do you know what Calvary was? What? What? What?" He said it like that, jerky, pressing his question. "Do you know what Calvary was?" Then, having waited a little and having walked up and down in front of them in silence, he looked at them again and said, "I'll tell you what Calvary was. It was *damnation*, and he took it *lovingly.*" The students in his class reported that there were tears in his eyes he said it. And well there might be. *"Damnation*, and he took it *lovingly!"*

Calvin's understanding of the clause of the creed which says "He descended into hell" was that it relates to the three hours of darkness on the cross, when the Son knew himself forsaken of his Father because he was bearing the world's sin. Probably that is not what the creed originally meant, but it is a good exposition of the truth about the cross. What love!

Deep, rich, and full peace of conscience comes only when you know that your sins have been not simply disregarded but judged, judged to the full and paid for to the full by the Son of God in your place.

Richard Hooker, that great Anglican theologian of the sixteenth century, wrote this at the end of his Learned *Sermon on Justification*. "Let men count it folly, or frenzy, or whatsoever. We care for no knowledge, no wisdom in the world but this, that man has sinned and God has suffered, that God has been made the sin of man and man is made the righteousness of God." My sin has been judged already, the penalty has been paid. "Payment God cannot twice demand, first from my bleeding surety's hand and then again from mine." This is the height of joy and glory, of thanksgiving, of almost overwhelming delight to which scriptural meditations on Christ's death as sacrifice and satisfaction lead us. "Thanks be to God for his indescribable gift" (2 Corinthians 9:15).

"Sacrifice and Satisfaction," pp. 135-37

When I survey the wondrous Cross
On which the Prince of glory died,
My richest gain I count but loss,
And pour contempt on all my pride.

See, from His head, His hands, His feet,
Sorrow and love flow mingled down;
Did e'er such love and sorrow meet,
Or thorns compose so rich a crown?

Were the whole realm of nature mine,
That were a tribute far too small;
Love so amazing, so divine,
Demands my soul, my life, my all.

-10-

His Giving Love

"Then Jesus declared, 'I am the bread of life. He who comes to me will never go hungry, and he who believes in me will never be thirsty. But as I told you, you have seen me and still you do not believe. All that the Father gives me will come to me, and whoever comes to me I will never drive away'" (John 6:35-37).

The theme of these verses is the greatest, sweetest, most glorious theme any preacher can ever handle: the love of God in Jesus Christ our Lord. It is the theme which Reformed people love to refer to as sovereign grace.

The love of God not only makes salvation possible but actually saves. It does more than create a possibility. It actually does the job.

These particular verses highlight the greatness, richness, sweetness, and glory of the truth of the love of God in Jesus our Lord because they show that the love of God not only makes salvation possible but actually saves. It does more than create a possibility. It actually does the job. The love of God is a far bigger, greater, and more wonderful thing than some Christians have yet seen.

How would you define the love of God if I put you on the spot and asked you to do so with reference to a text? I guess that you would go to John 3:16. I suppose that is about the best known text of the New Testament, and it does speak of the love of God in glowing terms. "God so loved the world that he gave his one and only Son, that whoever believes in him shall not perish but have eternal life." If you thought of quoting from the passage with which I began, you would perhaps cite verse 35, where Jesus says, "I am the bread of life. He who comes to me will never go hungry, and he who believes in me will never be thirsty." This too is a wonderful exhibition of the love of God. So we ask: What do these two texts show us?

First they show the love of God in *redemption*. In the sentence "God so loved the world that he gave," "gave" has reference to the cross of Christ. The words come just after Jesus has said to Nicodemus, "As Moses lifted up the snake in the desert, so the Son of Man must be lifted up." Once when Israel was traveling in the wilderness, snakes entered the camp, and the people were being bitten and were dying. God told Moses to make a brass snake, set it up in the middle of the camp, and tell any who were bitten by the snakes to look at the brass serpent and they would be cured. And so they were. This was a wonderful foreshadowing of the way in which we sinners may look to the representative "sinner"—yes, allow me to use that phrase, the One, I mean, who acts as a substitute for us sinners under the judgment of God— and be saved. There he is, lifted up on the cross. He is dying in our place. We look, see our sins judged there, and live. This is the beginning of the story of the love of God: redemption.

The second element in the love of God as revealed in Christ is *invitation*. These verses, John 3:16 and 6:35, also have this element, showing us that Jesus Christ, who died for sin, now opens his arms and invites us to come to him and promises to receive us as we come. "Come to me," he says, "and I will give you the fruits of my redemption. Come to me, and you will find through me the life you need. I am the bread of life. He who comes to me will never go hungry." The second half of verse 35 links up with that: "And he who believes in me will never be thirsty." Coming to Christ and believing on Christ are one thing. Each phrase explains the meaning of the other. In heart, one approaches him. In heart, one trusts him. In heart, one relies on him. In heart, one casts oneself upon him. This is believing. This is coming. "Closing with Jesus Christ"—that is the way Luther put it. He meant that one's faith is a kind of stretching out of one's arms to embrace Christ.

So the second element in the love of God in Christ our Lord is the risen Savior's invitation to those who need him and who know they need him to come, trust, and receive him and thereby to find life. Behind verse 35 one can hear the echo of the opening words of Isaiah 55: "Come, all you who are thirsty, come to the waters"—you who have no money, never mind—"come, buy and eat! Come, buy wine and milk without money and without cost."

Nor is this all. God's love towards us goes further. He works in our hearts by the agency of the Holy Spirit, taking away our imperviousness to his Word, taking away our inability to respond to that Word, and changing the disposition of our hearts so that instead of saying "Nonsense" when we hear the word of Christ, we say, "That's just what I need." And we come. "All that the Father gives me will come to me," says our Lord, because, as he said in verse 45, "it is written in the Prophets, 'They will all be taught by God.'" And he continues, "Everyone who listens to the Father and learns from him comes to me." So there is such a thing as divine teaching in the heart. There is such a thing as God enlightening people so that they receive and respond to Jesus' invitation. This is sometimes called irresistible grace, irresistible because it takes away the disposition to resist. As the Westminster Confession puts it, those who are the subjects of God's teaching, calling, drawing work come to Christ "most freely, being made willing by his grace."

Are you a Christian? A believer? Then you came to Christ because you found yourself willing, longing, desirous, wanting to, as well as, perhaps, not wanting to but knowing you must. How was that? It was because God worked in your heart to give you this desire. He changed you. It was his irresistible grace that drew you to the Savior's feet. Praise him for it! It was the supreme expression of his love to you.

"To All Who Come," p. 179, p. 183

ॐ

O the deep, deep love of Jesus,
Vast, unmeasured, boundless, free;
Rolling as a mighty ocean
In its fullness over me.
Underneath me, all around me,
'Tis the current of Thy love;
Leading onward, leading homeward,
To my glorious rest above.

-11-

His Saving Love

The saving ministry of Jesus Christ is summed up in the statement that he is the "mediator between God and men" (1 Timothy 2:5). A mediator is a go-between who brings together parties who are not in communication and who may be alienated, estranged, and at war with each other. The mediator must have links with both sides in order to identify with and maintain the interests of both and represent each to the other on a basis of good will.

In Calvin's words, "in an inconceivable way he loved us even when he hated us." God's gift to us of the Son as our sin bearer was the fruit of that love.

Every member of our fallen and rebellious race is by nature "hostile to God" (Romans 8:7) and stands under God's wrath (i.e., the punitive rejection whereby as Judge he expresses active anger at our sins, Romans 1:18; 2:5-9; 3:5-6). Reconciliation of the warring parties is needed, but this can occur only if God's wrath is somehow absorbed and quenched and man's anti-God heart, which motivates his anti-God life, is somehow changed. In mercy, God the angry Judge sent his Son into the world to bring about the needed reconciliation. It was not that the kindly Son acted to placate his harsh Father; the initiative was the Father's own. In Calvin's words, "in an inconceivable way he loved us even when he hated us." God's gift to us of the Son as our sin bearer was the fruit of that love (see John 3:14-16; Romans 5:5-8; 1 John 4:8-10). In all his mediatorial ministry the Son was doing his Father's will.

Objectively and once for all, Christ achieved reconciliation for us through penal substitution. On the cross he took our place; he carried our identity as it were, bore the curse due to us (see Galatians 3:13), and by his sacrificial blood-shedding made peace for us (see Ephesians 2:16; Colossians 1:20). *Peace* here means an end to hostility, guilt, and exposure to the retributive punishment that was otherwise unavoidable—in other words, pardon for all the past, and permanent personal acceptance for the future. Those who have received reconciliation through faith in Christ are justified and have peace with God (see Romans 5:1, 10). The mediator's present work, which he carries forward through human messengers, is to persuade those for whom he achieved reconciliation actually to receive it (see John 12:32; Romans 15:18; 2 Corinthians 5:18-21; Ephesians 2:17).

The three aspects of Christ's work are found together in the letter to the Hebrews, where Jesus is both the messianic King, exalted to his throne (1:3,13; 2:9; 4:16), and also the great High Priest (2:17; 4:14-5:10; chapters 7-10), who offered himself to God as a sacrifice for our sins. In addition, Christ is the messenger ("apostle," the one sent to announce, 3:1) through whom the message of which he is himself the substance was first spoken (2:3). In Acts 3:22 Jesus is called a prophet for the same reason that Hebrews calls him an apostle, namely, because he instructed people by declaring to them the Word of God.

While in the Old Testament the mediating roles of prophet, priest, and king were fulfilled by separate individuals, all three offices now coalesce in the one person of Jesus. It is his glory, given him by the Father, to be in this way the all-sufficient Savior. We who believe are called to understand this and to show ourselves his people by obeying him as our king, trusting him as our priest, and learning from him as our prophet and teacher. To center on Jesus Christ in this way is the hallmark of authentic Christianity.

Concise Theology, pp. 131-33

ॐ

Praise Him! Praise Him! Jesus, our blessed Redeemer!
Heav'nly portals loud with hosannas ring!
Jesus, Savior, reigneth forever and ever;
Crown Him! Crown Him! Prophet and priest and king!

Christ is coming, over the world victorious,
Pow'r and glory unto the Lord belong:

Praise Him! Praise Him!
Tell of His excellent greatness!
Praise Him! praise Him! ever in joyful song!

-12-

The Power of His Spirit

Before Jesus' passion, he promised that the Father and he would send his disciples "another Counselor" (John 14:16, 26; 15:26; 16:7). The Counselor or Paraclete, from the Greek word *parakletos* (meaning one who gives support), is a helper, adviser, strengthener, encourager, ally, and advocate. Another points to the fact that Jesus was the first Paraclete and is promising a replacement who, after he is gone, will carry on the teaching and testimony that he started (John 16:6-7).

Paraclete ministry, by its very nature, is personal, relational ministry, implying the full personhood of the one who fulfills it. Though the Old Testament said much about the Spirit's activity in Creation (e.g., Genesis 1:2; Psalm 33:6), revelation (e.g., Isaiah 61:1-6; Micah 3:8), enabling for service (e.g., Exodus 31:2-6; Judges 6:34; 15:14-15; Isaiah 11:2), and inward renewal (e.g., Psalm 51:10-12; Ezekiel 36:25-27), it did not make clear that the Spirit is a distinct divine Person. In the New Testament, however, it becomes clear that the Spirit is as truly a Person distinct from the Father as the Son is. This is apparent not only from Jesus' promise of "another Counselor," but also from the fact that the Spirit, among other things, speaks (Acts 1:16; 8:29; 10:19; 11:12; 13:2; 28:25), teaches (John 14:26), witnesses (John 15:26), searches (1 Corinthians 2:11), determines (1 Corinthians 12:11), intercedes (Romans 8:26-27), is lied to (Acts 5:3), and can be grieved (Ephesians 4:30). Only of a personal being can such things be said.

The Spirit, then, is "he," not "it," and he must be obeyed, loved, and adored along with the Father and the Son.

All God's work in us, touching our hearts, our characters, and our conduct, is done by the Spirit.

Witnessing to Jesus Christ, glorifying him by showing his disciples who and what he is (John 16:7-15), and making them aware of what they are in him (Romans 8:15-17; Galatians 4:6) is the Paraclete's central ministry. The Spirit enlightens us (Ephesians 1:17-18), regenerates us (John 3:5-8), leads us into holiness (Romans 8:14; Galatians 5:16-18), transforms us (2 Corinthians 3:18; Galatians 5:22-23), gives us assurance (Romans 8:16), and gifts us for ministry (1 Corinthians 12:4-11). All God's work in us, touching our hearts, our characters, and our conduct, is done by the Spirit, though aspects of it are sometimes ascribed to the Father and the Son, whose executive the Spirit is.

Concise Theology, pp. 143-45

For Thy Gift of God the Spirit,
With us, in us, e'er to be,
Pledge of life and Hope of glory,
Savior, we would worship Thee.

Moves to wake our souls from sleep.
Thrusts us through with sense of sin,
Then, Himself, the Pledge, He seals us,
Saving Advocate within.

He, the mighty God indwells us:
His to strengthen, help, empower;
His to overcome the Tempter,
Ours to call in danger's hour.

Father, grant Thy Holy Spirit
In our hearts may rule today,
Grieved not, quenched not, but unhindered
Hold us 'neath His mighty sway.

The Aspects of Grace

-13-
The Great Rescue

Salvation is a picture-word of wide application that expresses the idea of rescue from jeopardy and misery into a state of safety. The gospel proclaims that the God who saved Israel from Egypt, Jonah from the fish's belly, the psalmist from death, and the soldiers from drowning (Exodus 15:2; Jonah 2:9; Psalm 116:6; Acts 27:31), saves all who trust Christ from sin and sin's consequences.

As these earthly deliverances were wholly God's work, and not instances of people saving themselves with God's help, so it is with salvation from sin and death. "For it is by grace you have been saved, through faith—and this not from yourselves, it [either faith as such or salvation and faith together] is the gift of God" (Ephesians 2:8). "Salvation comes from the Lord" (Jonah 2:9).

What are believers saved from? From their former position under the wrath of God, the dominion of sin, and the power of death (Romans 1:18; 3:9; 5:21); from their natural condition of being mastered by the world, the flesh, and the devil (John 8:23-24; Romans 8:7-8; 1 John 5:19); from the fears that a sinful life engenders (Romans 8:15; 2 Timothy 1:7; Hebrews 2:14-15), and from the many vicious habits that were part of it (Ephesians 4:17-24; 1 Thessalonians 4:3-8; Titus 2:11-3:6).

How are believers saved from these things? Through Christ, and in Christ. The Father is as concerned to exalt the Son as he is to rescue the lost (John 5:19-23; Philippians 2:9-11; Colossians 1:15-18; Hebrews 1:4-14), and it is as true to say the elect were appointed for Christ the beloved Son as it is to say that Christ was appointed for the beloved elect (Matthew 3:17; 17:5; Colossians 1:13; 3:12; 1 Peter 1:20; 1 John 4:9-10).

Our salvation involves, first, Christ dying for us and, second, Christ living in us (John 15:4; 17:26; Colossians 1:27) and we living in Christ, united with him in his death and risen life (Romans 6:3-10; Colossians 2:12, 20; 3:1). This vital union, which is sustained by the Spirit from the divine side and by faith from our side, and which is formed in and through our new birth, presupposes covenantal union in the sense of our eternal election in Christ (Ephesians 1:4-6). Jesus was foreordained to be our representative head and substitutionary sin bearer (1 Peter 1:18-20; cf. Matthew 1:21), and we were chosen to be effectually called, conformed to his image, and glorified by the Spirit's power (Romans 8:11, 29-30).

Our salvation involves, first, Christ dying for us and, second, Christ living in us.

Believers are saved from sin and death, but what are they saved for? To live for time and eternity in love to God—Father, Son, and Spirit—and to their neighbors. The source of love for God is knowledge of God's redeeming love for us, and the evidence of love for God is neighbor-love (1 John 4:19-21). God's purpose, here and hereafter, is to keep expressing his love in Christ to us, and our goal must be to keep expressing our love to the three Persons of the one God by worship and service in Christ. The life of love and adoration is our hope of glory, our salvation now, and our happiness forever.

Concise Theology, pp. 146-48

And can it be that I should gain
An interest in the Savior's blood?
Died He for me, who caused His pain?
For me, who Him to death pursued?

Amazing love! How can it be
That Thou, my God, shouldst die for me?
Amazing love! How can it be
That Thou, my God, shouldst die for me?

No condemnation now I dread;
Jesus, and all in Him, is mine!
Alive in Him, my living Head,
And clothed in righteousness Divine,

Bold I approach the eternal throne,
And claim the crown, through Christ my own.
Bold I approach the eternal throne,
And claim the crown, through Christ my own.

-14-
Chosen, Called, Saved, and Kept

Redemption is through Christ, by his death. In Christ, says Paul, "we have redemption through his blood, the forgiveness of sins, in accordance with the riches of God's grace" (Ephesians 1:7). Redemption means a costly rescue from jeopardy; here, Paul pinpoints the jeopardy of guilt before God as that from which we are redeemed. In the same connection, he says elsewhere that we are justified by grace "through the redemption that came by Christ Jesus" (Romans 3:24; cf. Titus 3:7). Paul points us to the cross of Christ as both proof of the reality of God's grace and as the final measure of it: "God demonstrates his own love for us in this: While we were still sinners, Christ died for us" (Romans 5:8; cf. 1 John 4:8-10).

Regeneration is in Christ, by union with him in his resurrection. Paul expounds it as a co-quickening with Christ (see Ephesians 2:1, 5f.; Romans 6:4ff.; Colossians 2:12; 3:1ff.), and stresses that it springs from the mercy and grace of God alone (see Ephesians 2:4; Titus 3:5). Regeneration is the necessary complement of redemption, for without it there is no faith in the Redeemer, and therefore no benefit from his death. Part of the meaning of the spiritual "death" which is our natural state (see Ephesians 2:1,5; Colossians 2:13) is that we are impotent to turn to Christ in repentance and faith; part of the effect of regeneration, however, is that faith dawns in our hearts. So Paul writes:

71

"by grace you have been saved through faith; and this is not your own doing, it is the gift of God" (Ephesians 2:8). Whether "this" refers to faith simply, or to salvation-through-faith as a whole, is not quite certain, but on either view Paul is saying that faith springs from spiritual co-resurrection, with Christ (see the context), and that this co-resurrection, to which we ourselves contribute nothing, derives from God's initiative—it is a fruit of grace. Thus it appears that, as Luke says, men and women believe "by grace" (Acts 18:27) as God calls them by his grace (see Galatians 1:15).

From the election of sinners flow their redemption, regeneration, faith, and final glory.

Election in the New Testament is God's eternal, unconditional choice of guilty offenders to be redeemed and regenerated (called and justified, Romans 8:30), and so brought to glory (see Ephesians 1:3-12). It is a choice made in Christ (Ephesians 1:4), in the sense that it is a choice both of sinners to be saved in union with God's Son and of him to become man and be their Savior (cf. 1 Peter 1:20). Paul speaks of this choice as "the election of grace" (Romans 11:5), God's "purpose and grace, [which] was given us in Christ Jesus before the beginning of time" (2 Timothy 1:9). From the election of sinners flow their redemption, regeneration, faith, and final glory (see 2 Thessalonians 2:13f.). From the appointment of the Son as Savior flow his incarnation (see John 6:38), the cross and resurrection (see John 20:15-18), and the calling, drawing, and keeping of those whom he was sent to save until the final resurrection (see John 6:39f.; 10:27ff.; 12:32; 17:2).

Preservation is God keeping in Christ those whom he has united to Christ by faith through the Spirit. Paul shares with Christians his confidence that "he who began a good work in you will carry it on to completion until the day of Christ Jesus"

(Philippians 1:6), grounding this certainty on God's faithfulness to his plan, his promise, and his people (see 2 Thessalonians 3:3; cf. 1 Corinthians 1:8f.). In Romans 8:30 he spells out the plan: "those he predestined, he also called; those he called, he also justified; those he justified, he also glorified." The past tense of "glorified" argues that because it is fixed in the plan it is as good as done already; thus it is in effect a promise that it will certainly be done in due course. So Paul can say he is sure that God "is able to guard what I have entrusted to him for that day." Christ's own promise undergirds this confidence: "My sheep listen to my voice; I know them, and they follow me. I give them eternal life, and they shall never perish; no one can snatch them out of my hand" (John 10:27). *God's Words, pp. 100-102*

"Man of Sorrows," what a name
For the Son of God who came
Ruined sinners to reclaim!
Hallelujah! What a Savior!

Bearing shame and scoffing rude,
In my place condemned He stood;
Sealed my pardon with His blood:
Hallelujah! What a Savior!

Guilty, vile and helpless, we:
Spotless Lamb of God was He:
"Full atonement!" Can it be?
Hallelujah! What a Savior!

"Lifted up" was He to die,
"It is finished," was His cry;
Now in heav'n exalted high:
Hallelujah! What a Savior!

When He comes, our glorious King,
All His ransomed home to bring,
Then anew this song we'll sing:
Hallelujah! What a Savior!

-15-

Christ Paid the Debt That You Could Never Pay

Atonement means making amends, blotting out the offense, and giving satisfaction for wrong done; thus reconciling to oneself the alienated other and restoring the disrupted relationship.

Scripture depicts all human beings as needing to atone for their sins but lacking all power and resources for doing so. We have offended our holy Creator, whose nature it is to hate sin (see Jeremiah 44:4; Habakkuk 1:13) and to punish it (see Psalm 5:4-6; Romans 1:18, 2:5-9). No acceptance by, or fellowship with, such a God can be expected unless atonement is made, and since there is sin in even our best actions, anything we do in hopes of making amends can only increase our guilt or worsen our situation. This makes it ruinous folly to seek to establish one's own righteousness before God (see Job 15:14-16; Romans 10:2-3); it simply cannot be done.

Scripture depicts all human beings as needing to atone for their sins but lacking all power and resources for doing so.

But against this background of human hopelessness, Scripture sets forth the love, grace, mercy, pity, kindness, and compassion of God, the offended Creator, in himself providing the atonement that our sin has made necessary. This amazing grace is the focal center of New Testament faith, hope, worship, ethics, and spiritual life; from Matthew to Revelation it shines out with breathtaking glory.

New Testament references to the blood of Christ are regularly sacrificial (e.g., Romans 3:25; 5:9; Ephesians 1:7; Revelation 1:5). As a perfect sacrifice for sin (see Romans 8:3; Ephesians 5:2; 1 Peter 1:18-19), Christ's death was our redemption (i.e., our rescue by ransom: the paying of a price that freed us from the jeopardy of guilt, enslavement to sin, and expectation of wrath; Romans 3:24; Galatians 4:4-5; Colossians 1:14). Christ's death was God's act of reconciling us to himself, overcoming his own hostility to us that our sins provoked (see Romans 5:10; 2 Corinthians 5:18-19; Colossians 1:20-22). The Cross propitiated God (i.e., quenched his wrath against us by expiating our sins and so removing them from his sight). Key texts here are Romans 3:25; Hebrews 2:17; 1 John 2:2 and 4:10, in each of which the Greek expresses propitiation explicitly. The cross had this propitiatory effect because in his suffering Christ assumed our identity, as it were, and endured the retributive judgment due to us ("the curse of the law," Galatians 3:13) as our substitute, in our place, with the damning record of our transgressions nailed by God to his cross as the tally of crimes for which he was now dying (see Colossians 2:14; cf. Matthew 27:37; Isaiah 53:4-6; Luke 22:37).

Christ's atoning death ratified the inauguration of the new covenant, in which access to God under all circumstances is guaranteed by Christ's one sacrifice that covers all transgressions (see Matthew 26:27-28; 1 Corinthians 11:25; Hebrews 9:15; 10:12-18). Those who through faith in Christ have "received reconciliation" (Romans 5:11) "in him... become the righteousness of God" (2 Corinthians 5:21). In other words, they are justified and receive the status of adopted children in God's family (see Galatians 4:5). Thereafter they live under the motivating constraint and control of the love of Christ for them as made known and measured by the cross (2 Corinthians 5:14).

Concise Theology, pp. 134-36

From whence this fear and unbelief?
Has not the Father put to grief
His spotless Son for me?
And will the righteous Judge of men
Condemn me for that debt of sin
Which, Lord, was charged on thee?

Complete atonement thou hast made,
And to the utmost farthing paid
Whate'er thy people owed;
How then can wrath on me take place
When sheltered in thy righteousness
And sprinkled with thy blood?

Turn then, my soul, unto thy rest!
The merits of thy great High Priest
Have bought thy liberty;
Trust in his efficacious blood,
Nor fear thy banishment from God,
Since Jesus died for thee.

-16-
Growing in Family Likeness

What is sanctification? The root meaning of the word is relational or, as some say, positional. To sanctify, or consecrate, is to set something or someone apart for God, either in general and inclusive terms or for some specific purpose, and to have it, or him, or her, accepted by God for the end that is in view. So in Jesus' high-priestly prayer he says: "For them I sanctify myself, that they too may be truly sanctified" (John 17:19). Jesus' self-sanctification was the specific setting of himself apart to be the sacrifice for his disciples' sins; their sanctification, and ours, is the inclusive setting of ourselves apart to be God's holy people in every aspect, department, activity, and relationship of our lives.

But whereas Jesus' self-sanctification is his own act, he speaks of our sanctification as a work of God upon us and in us. This points us to the further truth that when God sets fallen human beings like ourselves apart for himself, to be his servants and worshipers and to live in fellowship with him, his action is transformational in its character and effects. Why so? Because those whom God sets apart for himself must be Godlike.

Regeneration is glorification in the seed, sanctification is glorification in the bud, and glorification in heaven is the full flower.

We are talking about God's work of character change in Christians; about the life of God in human souls; about the fruit of the Spirit; about the outworking in our behavior of the life—our new, supernatural life—that is hid in Christ with God. We are talking about God working in us to make us will and act for his good pleasure. We are talking about the family likeness that God the Father wants to see in all his adopted children—the family likeness that is Christlikeness, displaying the love, humility, and righteousness that constitute the moral image of the Son, who is himself the image of the holy Father. We are talking about God supernaturalizing our lives and causing us to behave in ways in which, left to our own resources, we never could have behaved. We are talking about an ongoing spiritual mystery. If regeneration is a work of new creation, sanctification is a work of new formation. If regeneration is a new birth, sanctification is a new growth. If regeneration means our Adamic nature nailed to the cross and Christ's risen life implanted, sanctification means our Adamic nature dying and Christ's life within us flowing. "Those he justified, he also glorified," said Paul (Romans 8:30). If regeneration is glorification in the seed, sanctification is glorification in the bud, and glorification in heaven is the full flower.

Hot Tub Religion, pp. 172-74

Breathe on me, Breath of God,
Fill me with life anew.
That I may love what Thou dost love,
And do what Thou wouldst do.

Breathe on me, Breath of God,
Until my heart is pure,
Until with Thee I will one will,
To do and to endure.

Breathe on me, Breath of God,
Till I am wholly Thine,
Till all this earthly part of me
Glows with Thy fire divine.

Breathe on me, Breath of God,
So shall I never die,
But live with Thee the perfect life
Of Thine eternity.

-17-
Desiring God and His Holiness

Sanctification, says the *Westminster Shorter Catechism* (Q.35), is "the work of God's free grace, whereby we are renewed in the whole man after the image of God, and are enabled more and more to die unto sin, and live unto righteousness." The concept is not of sin being totally eradicated (that is to claim too much) or merely counteracted (that is to say too little), but of a divinely wrought character change freeing us from sinful habits and forming in us Christlike affections, dispositions, and virtues.

Regeneration is birth; sanctification is growth.

Sanctification is an ongoing transformation within a maintained consecration, and it engenders real righteousness within the frame of relational holiness. Relational sanctification, the state of being permanently set apart for God, flows from the cross, where God through Christ purchased and claimed us for himself (Acts 20:28; 26:18; Hebrews 10:10). Moral renovation, whereby we are increasingly changed from what we once were, flows from the agency of the indwelling Holy Spirit (Romans 8:13; 12:1-2; 1 Corinthians 6:11, 19-20; 2 Corinthians 3:18; Ephesians 4:22-24; 1 Thessalonians 5:23; 2 Thessalonians 2:13; Hebrews 13:20-21). God calls his children to sanctity and graciously gives what he commands (1 Thessalonians 4:4; 5:23).

Regeneration is birth; sanctification is growth. In regeneration, God implants desires that were not there before: desire for God, for holiness, and for the hallowing and glorifying of God's name in this world; desire to pray, worship, love, serve, honor, and please God; desire to show love and bring benefit to others. In sanctification, the Holy Spirit "works in you to will and to act" according to God's purpose; what he does is prompt you to "work out your salvation" (i.e., express it in action) by fulfilling these new desires (Philippians 2:12-13). Christians become increasingly Christlike as the moral profile of Jesus (the "fruit of the Spirit") is progressively formed in them (2 Corinthians 3:18; Galatians 4:19; 5:22-25).

Regeneration was a momentary monergistic act of quickening the spiritually dead. As such, it was God's work alone. Sanctification, however, is in one sense synergistic—it is an ongoing cooperative process in which regenerate persons, alive to God and freed from sin's dominion (Romans 6:11, 14-18), are required to exert themselves in sustained obedience. God's method of sanctification is neither activism (self-reliant activity) nor apathy (God-reliant passivity), but God-dependent effort (2 Corinthians 7:1; Philippians 3:10-14; Hebrews 12:14). Knowing that without Christ's enabling we can do nothing, morally speaking, as we should, and that he is ready to strengthen us for all that we have to do (Philippians 4:13), we "stay put" (remain, abide) in Christ, asking for his help constantly—and we receive it (Colossians 1:11; 1 Timothy 1:12; 2 Timothy 1:7; 2:1).

The standard to which God's work of sanctifying his saints is directed is his own revealed moral law, as expounded and modeled by Christ himself. Christ's love, humility, and patience under pressure are to be consciously imitated (Ephesians 5:2; Philippians 2:5-11; 1 Peter 2:21), for a Christlike spirit and attitude are part of what law-keeping involves.

Believers find within themselves contrary urgings. The Spirit sustains their regenerate desires and purposes; their fallen, Adamic instincts (the "flesh") which, though dethroned, are not yet destroyed, constantly distract them from doing God's will and allure them along paths that lead to death (Galatians 5:16-17; James 1:14-15). To clarify the relationship between the law and sin, Paul analyzes in a personal and dramatic way the sense of impotence for complete law-keeping, and the enslavement to behavior one dislikes, that the Spirit-flesh tension produces (Romans 7:14-25). This conflict and frustration will be with Christians as long as they are in the body. Yet by watching and praying against temptation, and cultivating opposite virtues, they may through the Spirit's help "mortify" (i.e., drain the life out of, weaken as a means of killing) particular bad habits, and in that sense more and more die unto sin (Romans 8:13; Colossians 3:5). They will experience many particular deliverances and victories in their unending battle with sin, while never being exposed to temptations that are impossible to resist (1 Corinthians 10:13).

Concise Theology, pp. 169-71

O Jesus, I have promised
To serve thee to the end;
Be thou for ever near me,
My Master and my Friend;
I shall not fear the battle
If thou art by my side,
Nor wander from the pathway
If thou wilt be my Guide.

O let me feel thee near me;
The world is ever near;
I see the sights that dazzle,
The tempting sounds I hear;
My foes are ever near me,
Around me and within;
But, Jesus, draw thou nearer,
And shield my soul from sin.

Growth in Grace

ಶ

-18-
Growing Up in Christ

Last words are ordinarily solemn words. Here are Peter's last recorded words at the end of his second letter: "Grow in the grace and knowledge of our Lord and Savior Jesus Christ. To him be glory both now and forever! Amen."

The Christian life begins with new birth, and birth is meant to issue in growth.

I expect that you speak of spiritual growth often and that you think it is important. You are right. It is important. Why? This is not only because personal growth has become of great concern in the secular world these days, but chiefly because, as we know from the Bible, the growth of God's children is a central concern of God himself. The Christian life begins with new birth, and birth is meant to issue in growth.

In the New Testament, growth in grace is a *fact*. At the beginning of 2 Thessalonians, Paul is praising God for the way in which the Thessalonian believers had grown: "We ought always to thank God for you, brothers... because your faith is growing more and more, and the love every one of you has for each other is increasing" (2 Thessalonians 1:3).

We find further that growth in grace is a *goal* for which the apostles prayed, and to which they gave direction. In 1 Thessalonians 3:12, we find Paul praying for the same thing for which he was praising God at the beginning of the second letter. He prayed, "May the Lord make your love increase and overflow for each other and for everyone else." He prayed that they might increase in love, and he was seeing the answer to his prayers when he later praised God that they were, in fact, so increasing. Colossians 1:10 and Philippians 1:9-11 show Paul praying that believers might grow in faith and love and abound in good works. Peter, from whom we took the words with which we started, gave directions for growth at the beginning of his first letter, saying, "Like newborn babies, crave pure spiritual milk [that is, the Word of God], so that by it you may grow up in your salvation" (1 Peter 2:2).

Growing in grace is also *commanded*. "Grow in grace!" says Peter in the imperative mood. To grow in grace is not an option, but an order.

You know what joy it is to parents for the first few weeks to have a baby. But just imagine, if the months and years went by and the baby never grew. Imagine that at the end of, shall we say, five or ten years the baby was still eighteen inches long, lying helpless in a cradle, not having grown. No one would be rejoicing then. It would seem a tragedy. It is equally horrible when the children of God, newborn babes in Christ, fail to grow toward the stature of their Savior. As Arthur Pink once said, "It brings no glory to God that his children should be dwarfs."

"The Means of Growth," pp. 2-3

O Jesus Christ, grow thou in me,
And all things else recede;
My heart be daily nearer thee,
From sin be daily freed.

More of thy glory let me see,
Thou Holy, Wise and True;
I would thy living image be
In joy and sorrow too.

Fill me with gladness from above,
Hold me by strength divine;
Lord, let the glow of thy great love
Through my whole being shine.

Make this poor self grow less and less,
Be thou my life and aim;
make me daily, through thy grace,
More fit to bear thy name.

-19-
Living Out
What God Has Done

Three basic facts constitute the foundations of growth in grace. Fact number one is *regeneration by the Holy Spirit's new birth,* what Paul in Titus 3:5 calls "rebirth and renewal by the Holy Spirit." When people turn to God we call it conversion. But we know that God works in people to make them will and do of his good pleasure, and it is only because he so works that we do turn to God. So our turning to God in repentance and faith is equally God turning us to himself by the sovereign work and power of his Holy Spirit. When we think of this great change as our turning to God we call it conversion. When we think of it as God turning us to himself, we call it regeneration or new birth. Conversion and regeneration are then the same great change of direction, viewed, however, from two different angles. Not all post-Reformation theologians have said it quite like that. But John Owen, the Puritan, who of all English-speaking theologians seems to me the greatest, saw and expounded it that way. He has convinced me. He said that conversion is my action, psychologically speaking. But he added that it is equally God's work in me and that he must have all the praise and glory for it.

God's work of regeneration then, of which conversion is the psychological form, is the first foundation of growth in grace. Through regeneration we become new creatures, indwelt by the Holy Spirit, who wrought this great change in us. Growth in grace means going on from there; it is the living out, maturing, and ripening of what God wrought in us when he turned us to himself.

Alongside this first foundation is a second: *justification by grace*. Regeneration and justification—that is, our pardon and acceptance by God—are two facts which go together. The passage in which we find the phrase, "rebirth and renewal by the Holy Spirit" is really on justification. It begins in Titus 3:4. "When the kindness and love of God our Savior appeared, he saved us, not because of righteous things we had done [there were no such deeds], but because of his mercy. He saved us through the washing [that consists] of *rebirth* and *renewal by the Holy Spirit*, whom he poured out on us generously through Jesus Christ our Savior, so that, *having been justified by his grace*, we might become *heirs* having the hope of eternal life. This is a trustworthy saying" (vv. 4-8). You see the links here. With new birth goes justification. And with justification goes adoption into God's family and our instatement as God's heirs. Now, therefore, we are God's children. His law is now our family code and no longer an oppressive burden as it was before we were converted. It is now an expression of our Father's will which we delight to keep because we want to please the One who loved us and saved us. So it is for all who are justified, and growth in grace is growth into this glad obedience.

The third fact, which goes with the first two, is: *incorporation into Christ*. As Paul says in Galatians 3:27: "All of you who were baptized into Christ have clothed yourselves with Christ." Now we are in Christ, united to him for time and eternity. Again, he says in 1 Corinthians 12:13: "We were all baptized by one Spirit into one body [the body of Christ, which is the fellowship of all believing people]." Now we are members of Christ's body in the basic scriptural sense of being his limbs, for that is what "members" means in the New Testament: limbs, organs, parts in the body of Christ. The head, Christ, himself, animates and nourishes the whole so that the whole fellowship, as Paul said in Ephesians 4:16, "grows and builds itself in love." The believer's personal growth in grace is growth within the overall growth of the body. Christians ordinarily grow in a context of fellowship, not apart from that context.

Growing in grace means that this profile of the Savior becomes more and more what we are in our character, attitudes, and conduct.

Our individual growth in grace, which rests upon these three things, is that work of God in our lives that is pictured in 2 Corinthians 3:18—our being changed from glory to glory by the Lord who is the Spirit. We call it sanctification, but growth in grace is an equally proper name for it. It is the work of God in bringing forth in us what in Galatians 5:22 is called "the fruit of the Spirit... love, joy, peace, patience, kindness, goodness, faithfulness, gentleness and self-control." As we look at those qualities we realize that they are a profile of Jesus Christ in the lives of his followers. Growing in grace means that this profile of the Savior, this reflection of his lovely and glorious character, becomes more and more what we are in our character, attitudes, and conduct.

"The Means of Growth," pp. 3-5

Blessed assurance, Jesus is mine!
O what a foretaste of glory divine!
Heir of salvation, purchased of God,
Born of His Spirit, washed in His blood.

Perfect submission, all is at rest,
I in my Savior am happy and blest;
Watching and waiting, looking above,
Filled with His goodness, lost in His love.

This is my story, this is my song,
Praising my Savior all the day long;
This is my story, this is my song,
Praising my Savior all the day long.

-20-
Signs of Growth

When spiritual growth—growth in the graces of Christian character, and in intimacy with God—is taking place, one may expect to
see at least these signs of it:

1. Sign one is a growing delight in praising God, with an increasing distaste for being praised oneself. A purpose of praise runs
throughout the Bible. It roots itself in every Christian heart and
becomes, not necessarily more exuberant, but certainly more
emphatic, as the saint matures. And the higher one goes in praising God, the lower one will go in one's own eyes, and the more
passionately one's heart will cry, with the psalmist: "Not to us, O
Lord, not to us but to your name be the glory, because of your
love and faithfulness" (Psalm 115:1). When Christians feel this
way more and more strongly, it would seem that they are growing
in grace.

2. Sign two is a growing instinct for caring and giving, with a
more pronounced dislike of the self-absorption that constantly
takes without either caring or giving. Love, we have seen, is of the
essence of Christ likeness; and love is entirely a matter of caring
and giving. Jesus cared and gave without stint all through his
ministry. Even in the agony of his crucifixion we find him caring
and praying for his executioners, that they might be forgiven
(Luke 23:34); caring for his mother, and charging John to look
after her (John 19:26-27); and caring for the penitent thief, to

whom he promised salvation (Luke 23:43). When Christians become more committed to love, and more abhorrent of unlove in its various forms, it would seem that they are growing in grace.

3. Sign three is a growing passion for personal righteousness, with more acute distress at the godlessness and immorality of the world around, and a keener discernment of Satan's strategy of opposition, distraction, and deception for ensuring that people neither believe nor live right. "We are not unaware of his schemes," said Paul, with some grimness (2 Corinthians 2:11). Every Christian needs to be able to say the same. When Christians show more grief that God is being dishonored and provoked by behavior that he hates, and more realism about the spiritual warfare involved in rolling back the evil tide, and more care lest they be drawn into sin themselves, it would seem that they are growing in grace.

4. Sign four is a growing zeal for God's cause, with more willingness to take unpopular action to further it. This is not to defend foolish gestures, which will certainly be unpopular and deservedly so. Strategic and tactical wisdom, and mature understanding of the issues involved, are called for in any public action. "Praise to the Lord my Rock, who trains my hands for war," wrote David (Psalm 144:1). Similarly, Christians preparing to fight the Lord's battles for truth and life need God to train, in this case, their minds. When Christians humbly allow wisdom to temper their zeal and yet remain ready (more so than at one time) to lay themselves on the line in what in unmistakably God's cause, it would seem that they are growing in grace.

5. Sign five is a greater patience and willingness to wait for God and bow to his will, with a deeper abhorrence of what masquerades as the bold faith, but is really the childish immaturity, that tries to force God's hand. It is the way of children to want things now, and to say and feel most passionately that they cannot wait for them or do without them. But the adult way of petitioning is the way of submission, modeled by Jesus in Gethsemane—"My Father, if it is possible... Yet not as I will, but as you will" (Matthew 26:39). It is right to tell God what we long for and would like him to do, but it is also right to remind ourselves and acknowledge to him that he knows best. When Christians are learning to submit to God's ordering of events with undaunted realism and humility, it would seem that they are growing in grace.

Rediscovering Holiness, pp. 188-90

‹ð

Who is on the Lord's side? Who will serve the King?
Who will be His helpers, other lives to bring?
Who will leave the world's side? Who will face the foe?
Who is on the Lord's side? Who for Him will go?
By Thy call of mercy, by Thy grace divine,
We are on the Lord's side, Savior, we are Thine.

Not for weight of glory, not for crown and palm,
Enter we the army, raise the warrior psalm;
But for love that claimeth lives for whom He died;
He whom Jesus nameth must be on His side,
By Thy love constraining, by Thy grace divine,
We are on the Lord's side, Savior, we are Thine.

-21-
Being Remade

Every human individual has infinite worth, being made by God for nobility and glory; but every human individual is currently twisted out of moral shape in a way that only God can cure. To put it in standard Christian language, each of us by nature is God's image-bearer, but is also fallen and lives under the power of sin, and now needs grace. Sin is a sickness of the spirit, and the tragic sense of life, in inner tensions and contradictions, plus our inveterate unrealism, egoism, and indisposition to love God and our neighbor, are all symptoms of our disorder. Sometimes Christians have expressed this thought by saying that human beings, though good, are terribly weak. That, however, seems hardly adequate, and I side with those who speak more strongly and say that each of us is radically bad, though providentially kept from expressing our badness fully. But in human nature, viewed morally, as God views it, everything is out of tune to some extent. And though we have technology for straightening roads and integrating information, it is beyond us to straighten and integrate the human character. Man needs God for that.

The heart of the Christian message is that the Christ who exhibited in himself true and full humanness according to the Creator's intention, and who diagnosed the spiritual deformity that sin brings, and the personal disasters to which it leads, more trenchantly than was ever done before or since, died sacrificially to redeem us from sin; rose triumphantly from death; and now lives to forgive and remake us, and turn us by his power from the travesties of humanity that we really are into authentic human beings who bear his moral image. By his death and the forgiveness that flows from it he delivers us from God's condemnation; by leading us through his word in Scripture into the paths of discipleship, and by the transforming work of his Spirit at the level of our instincts, inclinations, insights, and attitudes (what Scripture calls our *heart*), he deprograms us from the game plans of our former ungodly self-centeredness, teaching us to look at everything through his eyes and literally to live a new life.

And though we have technology for straightening roads and integrating information, it is beyond us to straighten and integrate the human character. Man needs God for that.

Jesus Christ remakes us in his own moral and spiritual image, and this is something which we cannot do for ourselves by our own resources. I am further saying, therefore, that at some point along the line each of us must come to the point of admitting that we need to be saved, since we cannot save ourselves. We have not got what it takes to re-order our disordered lives; we need to be saved by Jesus Christ. It is those who in humble honesty reach that moment of truth who become Christians.

"A Christian View of Man," pp. 109-18

Years I spent in vanity and pride,
Caring not my Lord was crucified,
Knowing not it was for me He died
On Calvary.

O the love that drew salvation's plan!
O the grace that brought it down to man!
O the mighty gulf that God did span
At Calvary!

Mercy there was great and grace was free,
Pardon there was multiplied to me,
There my burdened soul found liberty
At Calvary.

-22-
The Means of Growth

What are the means of growth, the means whereby this work of God is carried on in your life and mine? Theological textbooks normally speak of "the means of grace," a medieval phrase that the reformers held on to in order to express the thought that through these particular activities God does work to transform our lives.

The means of grace are usually listed something like this: *Bible truth*, preached and received through preaching, studied in the text, meditated on, applied to oneself, taken to heart, laid up in the memory, taken as a guide for life; *prayer*, the regular exercise of communion and fellowship with God; *worship* with the Lord's people, particularly at the Lord's Supper but also in hearing the Word regularly proclaimed and joining in the prayers and the vocal praise; and the *informal fellowship* and interchange of the Lord's family as we stand by and minister to each other.

This is what it really means to grow in grace—that you do have your eyes on the Lord and your hope in the Lord all the time, and so are coming constantly to know him better.

As we approach the study of these growth activities, we need to remember first that growth which comes from God through these means comes only as in using them we look beyond them to the Lord himself, asking him to bless for our spiritual welfare what we are doing. If we suppose that sharing in these activities, "using the means of grace," as we say, has a magic of its own, if, that is, we suppose that we can trust the means of grace to guarantee our growth automatically, we will be off the track and will not grow in grace, however much we listen to sermons, pray, and go through the motions of fellowship with God spiritually, as opposed to using them superstitiously. *We are to grow precisely in the knowledge of our Lord and Savior Jesus Christ* to whom our eyes and our trust must be directed in everything. This is what it really means to grow in grace—that you do have your eyes on the Lord and your hope in the Lord all the time, and so are coming constantly to know him better.

Second, growth in grace is always growth by grace and under grace, never beyond grace. And grace means God enriching sinners. That is who we are. We do not grow beyond grace. We never get to a point where we can cease to thank God for Calvary on a day-to-day basis and humble ourselves before him as hell-deserving sinners. There is no sinless perfection in this life. Sinless perfection is part of the hope of glory. Here, the best the Lord enables us to do is less than perfect, and we must constantly ask God to forgive what is defective. Can you receive that insight? It is basic, I believe, to a true view of this matter. If you have understood the second half of Romans 7 where we see Paul at his best, reaching out after perfection and then lamenting that his reach exceeds his grasp, you will appreciate what I am saying. However much we use the means of grace, we shall never cease to be in this life hell-deserving sinners living daily by pardon. And God forbid that we should ever be found thinking in any other terms!

Real growth in grace will bring you consciously closer to Jesus Christ day by day, and that indeed will be one of the signs that God really is at work in your life. As you see him more clearly, love him more dearly, and follow him more nearly, you will grow in the knowledge of the One who is your Savior, sin bearer, example, master, and source of all the strength and power you need to follow in his steps.

God grant that we may grow in the grace and knowledge of Christ more and more every day of our lives.

"The Means of Growth," pp. 10-11

᷒

I need Thee every hour, most gracious Lord;
No tender voice like Thine can peace afford.

I need Thee every hour, stay Thou near by;
Temptations lose their power when thou art nigh.

I need Thee every hour, in joy or pain;
Come quickly and abide, or life is vain.

I need Thee every hour, most holy One;
O make me Thine indeed, Thou blessed Son.

I need Thee, O, I need Thee; every hour I need Thee!
O bless me now, my Savior, I come to Thee!

Trouble on
the Road to Glory

❧

-23-
Pain: God's Chisel for Sculpting Our Souls

Why does God not root indwelling sin out of his saints in the first moment of their Christian life, as he will do the moment they die? Why, instead, does he carry on their sanctification with a painful slowness, so that all their lives they are troubled by sin and never reach the perfection they desire? Why is it his custom to give them a hard passage through this world?

> *Christlike habits of action and reaction are ingrained most deeply as we learn to maintain them through experiences of pain and unpleasantness, which in retrospect appear as God's chisel for sculpting our souls.*

The answer is that he does all this for his glory—to expose to us our own weakness and impotence, so that we may learn to depend upon his grace and the limitless resources of his saving power. "We have this treasure in earthen vessels," wrote Paul, "that the excellency of the power may be of God, and not of us" (2 Corinthians 4:7, KJV). Once for all, let us rid our minds of the idea that things are as they are because God cannot help it. God "works out everything in conformity with the purpose of his will" (Ephesians 1:11), and all things are as they are because God has chosen that they should be, and the reason for his choice in every case is his glory.

When children are allowed to do what they like and are constantly shielded from situations in which their feelings might get hurt, we describe them as spoiled. When we say that, we are saying that over-indulgent parenthood not only makes them unattractive today but also fails to prepare them for the moral demands of adult life tomorrow—two evils for the price of one. But God, who always has his eye on tomorrow as he deals with us today, never spoils his children, and the lifelong training course in holy living in which he enrolls us challenges and tests us to the utmost again and again. Christlike habits of action and reaction—in other words, the fruit of the Spirit, love, joy, peace, patience, kindness, goodness, faithfulness, gentleness, and self-control (Galatians 5:22ff.)—are ingrained most deeply as we learn to maintain them through experiences of pain and unpleasantness, which in retrospect appear as God's chisel for sculpting our souls. There is more to sanctification than this, but not less. "Endure hardship as discipline; God is treating you as sons," writes the author of Hebrews. "For what son is not disciplined by his father? If you are not disciplined (and everyone undergoes discipline), then you are illegitimate children and not true sons" (Hebrews 12:7-8). Bastard offspring notoriously go uncared for, but, says the writer, it will not be so for you who believe. Your heavenly Father loves you enough to school you in holy living. Appreciate what he is doing, and be ready for the rough stuff that his program for you involves.

So any form of the idea that since God really loves us he must intend to keep us, or immediately to deliver us, out of all the troubles that threaten—poor health, lonely isolation, family disruption, shortage of funds, hostility, cruelty, or whatever—should be dismissed as utterly wrong. Faithful Christians will experience help and deliverance in times of trouble over and over again. But our lives will not be ease, comfort, and pleasure all the way. Burrs under the saddle and thorns in our bed will abound.

Hot Tub Religion, pp. 34-36, 77-78

Be still my soul! The Lord is on thy side;
Bear patiently the cross of grief or pain;
Leave to thy God to order and provide;
In every change He faithful will remain.
Be still, my soul! Thy best, thy heavenly Friend
Through thorny ways leads to a joyful end.

Be still, my soul! Thy God doth undertake
To guide thy future as He has the past;
Thy hope, thy confidence let nothing shake—
All now mysterious shall be bright at last.
Be still, my soul! The waves and winds still know
His voice who ruled them while He dwelt below.

Be still, my soul! The hour is hast'ning on
When we shall be forever with the Lord,
When disappointment, grief, and fear are gone,
Sorrow forgot, love's purest joys restored.
Be still, my soul! When change and tears are past,
All safe and blessed we shall meet at last.

-24-
In God's Hospital

We are all invalids in God's hospital. In moral and spiritual terms we are all sick and damaged, diseased and deformed, scarred and sore, lame and lopsided, to a far, far greater extent than we realize. Under God's care we are getting better, but we are not yet well. The modern Christian likes to dwell on present blessings rather than future prospects. Modern Christians egg each other on to testify that where once we were blind, deaf, and indeed dead so far as God was concerned, now through Christ we have been brought to life, radically transformed, and blessed with spiritual health. Thank God, there is real truth in that. But spiritual health means being holy and whole. To the extent that we fall short of being holy and whole, we are not fully healthy either.

Christians today can imagine themselves to be strong, healthy, and holy when, in fact, they are actually weak, sick, and sinful in ways that are noticeable not just to their heavenly Father, but also to their fellow believers. Pride and complacency, however, blind us to this reality. We decline to be told when we are slipping; thinking we stand, we set ourselves up to fall, and predictably, alas, we do fall.

In good hospitals, patients receive regular curative treatment as well as constant care, and the treatment determines in a direct way the form that the care will take. In God's hospital the course of treatment that the Father, Son, and Holy Spirit, the permanent medical staff (if I dare so speak), are giving to each of us with a view to our final restoration to the fullness of the divine image, is

115

called *sanctification*. It is a process that includes on the one hand medication and diet (in the form of biblical instruction and admonition coming in various ways to the heart), and on the other hand tests and exercises (in the form of internal and external pressures, providentially ordered, to which we have to make active response). The process goes on as long as we are in this world, which is something that God decides in each case.

The truth is that God knows what he is doing, but sometimes, for reasons connected with the maturity and ministry that he has in view for us, he makes haste slowly.

Like patients in any ordinary hospital, we are impatient for recovery. The question that forms the title of Lane Adams' wonderful little book on God's sanctifying therapy, *How Come It's Taking Me So Long to Get Better?*, is often our heart-cry to God. The truth is that God knows what he is doing, but sometimes, for reasons connected with the maturity and ministry that he has in view for us, he makes haste slowly. That is something we have to learn humbly to accept. We are in a hurry; he is not.

Rediscovering Holiness, pp. 40-42

Just a closer walk with thee,
Grant it, Jesus, is my plea;
Daily walking close to thee;
Let it be, dear Lord, let it be.

Through this world of toils and snares,
If I falter, Lord, who cares?
Who with me my burden shares?
None but thee, dear Lord, none but thee.

I am weak, but thou art strong.
Jesus, keep me from all wrong;
I'll be satisfied as long
As I walk, let me walk, close to thee.

-25-
Three Mistakes to Avoid

God's people sometimes make mistakes when thinking about spiritual growth. Here are three. Mistake number one: to *suppose that growth in grace is measurable* in the way that physical growth is measurable.

There is a divine mystery in the work by which God makes us grow in grace. We cannot measure it by any simple, regular technique of assessment like measuring height or checking weight. Growth in grace is known by the way we behave under pressure, when times of testing and temptation come, when the heat is on and there is a crisis. Then our reaction and behavior show whether we have been growing in grace or not.

Let me show what I mean from Scripture. Here is Abraham. At the age of seventy-five he was promised a son. He has waited eleven years, and now is eighty-six and his wife is only a few years younger. They cannot wait any longer. Their faith cracks. Sarah says to Abraham, "Look, I shall never have a child. You go have a son by Hagar, my maid, and then that child will count as ours, and thus the promised heir will appear." Thus Abraham and Sarah conspired together to play the amateur province and bring God's promise to pass by unhallowed means. And they did it! Ishmael was born. But God never accepted Ishmael. It was just a sad mistake, a testimony to immaturity in the life of faith and grace.

But follow the story on a little. Isaac has arrived—his parents being about one hundred years old at the time—and Isaac is now a teenager, while Abraham is a very elderly man indeed. Now we read in Genesis 22: "God tested Abraham. He said to him, 'Abraham... take your son, your only son Isaac, whom you love, and go to the region of Moriah. Sacrifice him there as a burnt offering'" (vv. 1, 2). Do you suppose that ever a father's heart hurt more than Abraham's heart hurt as he tramped up the mountain with Isaac? Do you suppose that any servant of God has ever felt more strongly, "This word from God is crazy"? Hardly. But Abraham had grown over the years, and this time he trusted God to know what he was doing. He was prepared at God's command to endure even the death of his son. This is the behavior of a man who has ripened in grace.

Now for mistake number two, which is to suppose that growth in grace is a uniform process. It is not so. There are growing times, when a person grows in the Lord much more rapidly than at other times. God, who finds us all different from each other when his grace first touches us, deals with different Christians in different ways.

Consider Peter. When Jesus called Peter he was a bluff, hearty, warmhearted, openhanded leadership type, as we would say. But he had one area of weakness. He was impulsive, headstrong, and unstable. On the evening of Jesus' betrayal he said to the Lord, "Though they all forsake you, I won't." But within a few hours of saying that, he was thrown into panic by a servant girl's questions and denied his master three times.

But now the crucified Jesus rises, ascends to heaven, and pours out the Spirit. What happens? From the day of Pentecost onward Peter is a transformed man. Very suddenly, at the point of his greatest weakness, he has grown. Now what he says is wise and weighty, and he is the anchor man of the early church, the real rock man. (*Petros* means "rock.") Oh, he still made mistakes. Paul calls attention to one of them in Galatians 2. But in the making of his character there had been a sudden and dramatic advance.

It is a triumph of grace when a person like Peter, who was unstable as water before Pentecost, is suddenly turned into a strong, steady man, which by nature he never could have been. What do you find yourself able to do through Christ today which you were never able to do before? If you have an answer to that question, you have a testimony to a real measure of growth in grace.

Growth in grace means, among other things, that you are becoming more richly and robustly human than you were before.

Mistake number three is to suppose *that growth in grace is automatic,* something you need not bother about because it will look after itself, something which is guaranteed, particularly if you are a professional minister, missionary, or church officer. The enemy wants to encourage all who seek to serve God to take it for granted that as we do our job we shall automatically grow and mature in Christ and therefore need not bother about sanctification at all. He wants to encourage us to think this way because, if we are not striving to grow, we are actually in danger of doing the very opposite, namely, shrinking as persons behind the roles we play.

Growth in grace means, among other things, that you are becoming more richly and robustly human than you were before. That is at the heart of what it means to be changed from one degree of glory to another, so that more and more you will come to bear the image of Jesus Christ, the perfect man.

"The Means of Growth," pp. 5-8

The God of Abraham praise, Who reigns enthroned above;
Ancient of everlasting days, and God of love.
Jehovah, great I AM, by earth and heav'n confessed;
I bow and bless the sacred name, forever blest.

The God of Abraham praise, at Whose supreme command
From earth I rise, and seek the joys at His right hand.
I all on earth forsake, its wisdom, fame, and power;
And Him my only portion make, my shield and tower.

He by Himself hath sworn, I on His oath depend,
I shall, on eagles' wings upborne, to heaven ascend;
I shall behold His face, I shall His power adore,
And sing the wonders of His grace forevermore.

-26-
Glorify God in Your Suffering

What is God's ultimate end in his dealings with his children? Is it simply their happiness, or is it something more? The Bible indicates that it is something more. It is the glory of God himself.

God's end in all his acts is ultimately himself. There is nothing morally dubious about this. If we say that man can have no higher end than the glory of God, how can we say anything different about God himself? The idea that it is somehow unworthy to represent God as aiming at his own glory in all that he does reflects a failure to remember that God and man are not on the same level. It shows lack of realization that, while sinful man makes his own well-being his ultimate end at the expense of his fellow creatures, our gracious God has determined to glorify himself by blessing his people. His end in redeeming man, we are told, is "the praise of his glorious grace," or simply "the praise of his glory" (Ephesians 1:6, 12, 14). He wills to display his resources of mercy (the "riches" of his grace, and of his glory—"glory" being the sum of his attributes and powers as he reveals them: Ephesians 2:17; 3:16) in bringing his saints to their ultimate happiness in the enjoyment of himself.

How does this truth, that God seeks his own glory in all his dealings with us, bear on the problem of providence? In this way: It gives us insight into the way in which God saves us, suggesting to us the reason why he does not take us to heaven the moment we believe. We now see that he leaves us in a world of sin to be tried, tested, belabored by troubles that threaten to crush us—in order that we may glorify him by our patience under suffering, and in order that he may display the riches of his grace and call forth new praises from us as he constantly upholds and delivers us. Psalm 107 is a majestic declaration of this.

Is it a hard saying? Not to the man who has learned that his chief end in this world is to "glorify God, and [in doing so] to enjoy him forever." The heart of true religion is to glorify God by patient endurance and to praise him for his gracious deliverances. It is to live one's life, through smooth and rough places alike, in sustained obedience and thanksgiving for mercy received.

> *The heart of true religion is to seek and find one's deepest joy, not in spiritual lotus-eating, but in discovering through each successive storm and conflict the mighty adequacy of Christ to save.*

It is to seek and find one's deepest joy, not in spiritual lotus-eating, but in discovering through each successive storm and conflict the mighty adequacy of Christ to save. It is the sure knowledge that God's way is best, both for our own welfare and for his glory. No problems of providence will shake the faith of the one who has truly learned this.

Hot Tub Religion, pp. 24-26

To God be the glory, great things He hath done,
So loved He the world that He gave us His Son,
Who yielded His life an atonement for sin,
And opened the Life Gate that all may go in.

Praise the Lord! Praise the Lord! Let the earth hear His voice!
Praise the Lord! Praise the Lord! Let the people rejoice!
Oh come to the Father, through Jesus the Son,
And give Him the glory—great things He has done.

Saying Yes to New Life

෴

-27-
Consecrating Yourself to God

What is consecration? It is the flip side of repentance. In repentance one turns away to God from what is wrong; in consecration one gives oneself to God for what is right. Both terms express the same "no" to the siren-songs of sin and the same "yes" to the saving call of Christ.

Through the Holy Spirit's agency, we become like the One we look at as we absorb the gospel word.

What is this transformation? It is the change into Christlikeness of which Paul speaks in 2 Corinthians 3:18. The New American Standard Version (NAS) renders very accurately thus: "All of us, with unveiled faces, seeing the glory of the Lord as though reflected in a mirror, are being transformed into the same image from one degree of glory to another." Through the Holy Spirit's agency, we become like the One we look at as we absorb the gospel word. Each step in this character-change (for conformity of character is what Paul is talking about) is a new degree of glory, that is, of God's self-display in our human lives.

How are the consecration and the transformation linked? Paul explains this in Romans 12:1-2, which the New International Version renders thus:

Therefore [as your way of glorifying God for his grace: see Romans 11:36], I urge you, brothers, in view of God's mercy [which has laid the groundwork for the gratitude we must now show], to offer your bodies [not bodies as opposed to souls, but your entire selves, body and soul, as in Philippians 1:20] as living sacrifices, holy [consecrated] and pleasing [a delight] to God—which is your spiritual worship. Do not conform any longer to the pattern of this world, but be transformed by the renewing of your mind [your heart, your desires, your thoughts and purposes, your entire inner life].

Paul's thought is that by our self-offering, we open ourselves to God, and thereby bring to an end any resistance to the indwelling Holy Spirit that may have been in us before. As a result the planned and promised supernaturalizing of our inner life through our sharing in Christ's risen life will proceed unhindered. "Then you will be able to test and approve [in each situation] what God's will is—his good, pleasing and perfect will" (v. 2). "Test and approve" renders a single Greek verb that means "discern through examining alternatives." The renewed mind, enlightened by the Spirit, and tuned by regeneration to seek God's glory, will compare the options and thereby perceive what course of action will best please God.

Rediscovering Holiness, pp. 171-72

We come, O Christ, to Thee, true Son of God and man,
By Whom all things consist, in Whom all life began:
In Thee alone we live and move,
And have our being in Thy love.

Thou art the Way to God, thy blood our ransom paid;
In Thee we face our Judge and Maker unafraid.
Before the throne absolved we stand:
Thy love has met Thy law's demand.

Thou only art true Life, to know Thee is to live
The more abundant life that earth can never give:
O risen Lord! We live in Thee
And Thou in us eternally!

We worship Thee, Lord Christ, our Savior and our King;
To Thee our youth and strength adoringly we bring:
So fill our hearts that men may see
Thy life in us, and turn to Thee!

-28-
Living a Life Worthy

The New Testament explains to us the newness of our life in Christ as a real and radical alteration of our personal being. It tells us that believers have been united to Christ, and are now "in" him, having died (finished with their old life) and been raised (started off in a new life) with their Lord (Romans 6:3-11; Ephesians 2:4-10; Colossians 2:11-14). In Christ they enjoy a new status. They are:

justified (pardoned and accepted);

adopted (made God's children and heirs); and

cleansed (fitted for fellowship with their holy Creator).

All aspects of their new status become real by virtue of Christ's suffering for them on the cross (see Romans 3:21-26; 5:1; 8:15-29; Galatians 4:4-7; John 15:3; 1 John 1:3-7). This is momentous. To be justified means that, by God's own judicial decision, I stand before him now and forever "just as if I had never sinned." To be adopted means that now I may call my Creator-Judge "Father," in the intimacy of his beloved family, and know myself to be an heir of his glory—"heirs of God and co-heirs with Christ" (Romans 8:17). To be cleansed means that nothing in my past imposes any restraint on my fellowship with God in the present.

Nor is that all. In Christ believers are also involved in a process of character change. The Holy Spirit (through whose agency faith was engendered in them) and Christ (through whom the new life was won for them, became consciously real to them) now indwell them to transform them "into his (Christ's) likeness with ever-increasing glory." Christ and his Spirit empower them to put sinful habits to death and bring forth in them the new behavior patterns that constitute the Spirit's "fruit" (see Romans 8:9-13; 2 Corinthians 3:18; Galatians 5:22-26). This, too, is momentous.

We who believe have to wake up to the fact that the ministry to us of the Father and the Son through the Spirit has turned us into different people from what we were by nature. Our present task is, as it is sometimes put, to be what we are—to live out what God has wrought in us, expressing in action the new life (new vision, motivation, devotion, and sense of direction) that has now become ours. Or, as Paul puts it, "Live a life worthy of the calling you have received" (Ephesians 4:1). The thought is the same.

We who believe have to wake up to the fact that the ministry to us of the Father and the Son through the Spirit has turned us into different people from what we were by nature.

Rediscovering Holiness, pp. 54-55

Take my life, and let it be
Consecrated, Lord, to thee.
Take my moments and my days;
Let them flow in ceaseless praise.

Take my hands, and let them move
At the impulse of thy love.
Take my feet, and let them be
Swift and beautiful for thee.

Take my voice, and let me sing
Always, only, for my King.
Take my lips, and let them be
Filled with messages from thee.

Take my will, and make it thine;
It shall be no longer mine.
Take my heart, it is thine own;
It shall be thy royal throne.

Take my love; my Lord, I pour
At thy feet its treasure-store.
Take myself, and I will be
Ever, only, all for thee.

-29-
How Can I Repay the Lord?

The plan of salvation teaches me, not merely that I can never do anything to earn, increase, or extend God's favor, or to avoid the justified fury of his wrath, or to wheedle benefits out of him, but also that I never need to try to do any of these things. God himself has loved me from eternity. He himself has redeemed me from hell through the cross. He himself has renewed my heart and brought me to faith. He himself has now sovereignly committed himself to complete the transformation of me into Christ's likeness and to set me, faultless and glorified, in his own presence for all eternity. When almighty love has thus totally taken over the task of getting me home to glory, responsive love, fed by gratitude and expressed in thanksgiving, should surface spontaneously as the ruling passion of my life. It will be my wisdom to brood on and mull over the marvelous mercies of God's plan until it does.

A little verse once taught to teenagers tells me where I ought to be in my response:

> I will not work my soul to save,
> For that my Lord has done;
> But I will work like any slave
> For love of God's dear Son.

Christians, says Paul, are to be moved and stirred to consecrated living by their knowledge of God's love, grace, and mercy—the mercy of sovereign salvation, whereby God pardons, accepts, and exalts the undeserving and wretched, at fearsome cost to himself. Insofar as there is a difference of nuance between the terms love, grace, and mercy of God, love means his outgoing to bless those whom he sees as having no claim on him; grace means his outgoing to bless those whom he sees as meriting his rejection; and mercy means his outgoing to bless those whose state he sees to be miserable. Love expresses God's self-determining freedom, grace his self-generated favor, and mercy his compassionate kindness. Paul has dwelt on God's sovereign mercy to sinners in Romans 9:15-18; 11:30-32. Now he says, in effect: "You who know this mercy in your own lives must show yourselves truly grateful for it by the thoroughness of your commitment to God henceforth. This thoroughness is your holiness, for holiness means giving your all to God as God has given, is giving, and will give his all to you. And this thoroughness will please God, for it will show your appreciation and affection for him, and so will be the real essence, Spirit-taught and Spirit-wrought, of your worship of him."

> *When almighty love has thus totally taken over the task of getting me home to glory, responsive love, fed by gratitude and expressed in thanksgiving, should surface spontaneously as the ruling passion of my life.*

It is important to be clear that, as praise to God for his transcendent greatness is the doxological basis of holiness, so commitment to spend one's life expressing gratitude to God's grace, every way one can, is its devotional basis.

The holy sacrifice that gives God pleasure is the Christian whose heart never ceases to be grateful to him for his grace. God is pleased with the Christian whose aim every day is to express that gratitude by living to him, through him, and for him, and who is constantly asking, with the psalmist, "How can I repay the Lord for all his goodness to me?" (Psalm 116:12).

Rediscovering Holiness, pp. 75-77

The love of God is greater far
Than tongue or pen can ever tell;
It goes beyond the highest star,
And reaches to the lowest hell.
The guilty pair, bowed down with care,
God gave His Son to win;
His erring child He reconciled,
And pardoned from his sin.

Could we with ink the ocean fill,
And were the skies of parchment made,
Were every stalk on earth a quill,
And every man a scribe by trade;
To write the love of God above
Would drain the ocean dry;
Nor could the scroll contain the whole,
Though stretched from sky to sky.

-30-
Just Say "No" to Sin

Holiness means, among other things, forming good habits, breaking bad habits, resisting temptations to sin, and controlling yourself when provoked. No one ever managed to do any of these things without effort and conflict.

How do we form the Christlike habits which Paul calls the fruit of the Spirit? By setting ourselves, deliberately, to do the Christlike thing in each situation. "Sow an act, reap a habit; sow a habit, reap a character." That might sound very simple and straightforward, but in practice it does not prove so. The test, of course, comes when the situation provokes us to cut loose with some form of ungodly tit-for-tat.

> *Your sin does not want to die, nor will it enjoy the killing process.*

We should think out our behavioral strategy with such situations directly in view. Thus, we should think of:

- *love* as the Christlike reaction to people's malice;
- *joy* as the Christlike reaction to depressing circumstances;
- *peace* as the Christlike reaction to troubles, threats, and invitations to anxiety;
- *patience* as the Christlike reaction to all that is maddening;
- *kindness* as the Christlike reaction to all who are unkind;

- *goodness* as the Christlike reaction to bad people and bad behavior;
- *faithfulness* and gentleness as the Christlike reaction to lies and fury; and
- *self-control* as the Christlike reaction to every situation that goads you to lose your cool and strike out.

The principle is clear, the Spirit is with us to empower us, and we know that Christlike behavior is now in the profoundest sense natural to us. But still, maintaining Christlikeness under the kind of pressures I have described is hard.

How do we "by the Spirit... put to death the misdeeds of the body" (Romans 8:13)? This too is hard. It is a matter of negating, wishing dead, and laboring to thwart, inclinations, cravings, and habits that have been in you (if I may put it so) for a long time. Pain and grief, moans and groans, will certainly be involved, for your sin does not want to die, nor will it enjoy the killing process. Jesus told us, very vividly, that mortifying a sin could well feel like plucking out an eye or cutting off a hand or foot, in other words, self-mutilation. You will feel you are saying good-bye to something that is so much part of you that without it you cannot live.

Both Paul and Jesus assure us that the exercise, however painful, is a necessity for life, so we must go to it (Matthew 5:29; 18:8; Romans 8:13). How? Outward acts of sin come from inner sinful urges, so we must learn to starve these urges of what stimulates them (porn magazines, for instance, if the urge is lust; visits to smorgasbords, if the urge is gluttony; gamblings and lotteries, if the urge is greed; and so on). And when the urge is upon us, we must learn, as it were, to run to our Lord and cry for help, asking him to deepen our sense of his own holy presence and redeeming love, to give us the strength to say "no" to that which can only displease him. It is the Spirit who moves us to act this way, who makes our sense of the holy love of Christ vivid, who imparts the strength for which we pray, and who actually drains the life out of the sins we starve.

Rediscovering Holiness, pp. 174-75

When we walk with the Lord
In the light of His Word,
What a glory he sheds on our way!
While we do His good will,
He abides with us still,
And with all who trust and obey.

Trust and obey
For there's no other way
To be happy in Jesus
But to trust and obey.

But we never can prove
The delights of His love
Until all on the altar we lay;
For the favor He shows
And the joy He bestows
Are for them who will trust and obey.

Then in fellowship sweet
We will sit at His feet
Or we'll walk by His side in the way;
What He says we will do,
Where He sends we will go;
Never fear, only trust and obey.

-31-
Nothing Can Dash You from His Hand

The Christian under grace is freed from the hopeless necessity of trying to commend himself to God by perfect law-keeping. Now he lives by being forgiven, and so is free at every point in his life to fail (as inevitably he does in fact, again and again)—and, having failed, to pick himself up where he fell, to seek and find God's pardon, and to start again. Pride, our natural disposition, which is self-protective, self-righteous, and vainglorious, will either refuse to admit failure at all or refuse to try again, lest the trauma of failing be repeated; but the humility of the man who lives by being forgiven knows no such inhibitions. The Christian's experience of daily failures, along with his inside knowledge of his own false motives and his tally of shameful memories, make him constantly want to claim for himself Paul's end-of-life self-description, "the worst of sinners" (1 Timothy 1:16); daily, however, his shortcomings are forgiven and his joy restored.

The Christian under grace is free from sin's dominion (see Romans 6:14). By virtue of his union with Christ, dead and risen, and the power of the Holy Spirit who indwells him, the Christian is able to oppose and resist the urgings to sin that infect his moral and spiritual system, and "by the Spirit... put to death the deeds of the body [the phrase means bad habits, whether of commission or omission]" (Romans 8:13), and so to advance in Christlikeness (cf. 2 Corinthians 3:18) and please God. Paul succinctly spells this out in Romans 6:1-8:14, arranging his thoughts as an answer to the question, "why should not those who are justified by faith cause grace to abound (pardoning grace, that is) by going on sinning as before?" Paul's reply, in brief, is: not only is righteousness (law-keeping) both possible and prescribed for Christians, but it is also a fact that no Christian can go on sinning as before, for union with Christ has changed his nature so that now his heart (his inner man) desires righteousness as before it desired sin, and only obedience to God can satisfy his deepest inner craving. He hates the sin that he finds in himself, and gets no pleasure from lapsing into it. Such is the state of mind of the man who is freed from sin's dominion; he loves holiness because he loves his Savior-God, and would not contemplate reverting to the days when, as sin's slave, he loved neither. He knows that his freedom has ennobled him and brought him both the desire and the strength for right living, and for this he is endlessly thankful.

The Christian under grace is free.

The Christian under grace is free from bondage to fear (see Romans 8:15ff.; cf. 1 John 4:17f.)—fear, that is, of the unknown future, or of meeting God (as one day we all must do), or of being destroyed by hostile forces or horrific experiences of one sort or another. He knows himself to be God's child, adopted, beloved, secure, with his inheritance awaiting him and eternal joy guaranteed. He knows that nothing can separate him from the love of God in Christ, nor dash him from his Savior's hand, and that nothing can happen to him which is not for his long-term good, making him more like Jesus and bringing him ultimately closer to his God.

God's Word, pp. 106-107

Jesus, I am resting, resting
In the joy of what Thou art:
I am finding out the greatness
Of Thy loving heart.
Thou hast bid me gaze upon Thee,
And Thy beauty fills my soul,
For by Thy transforming power,
Thou hast made me whole.

O, how great Thy lovingkindness,
Vaster, broader than the sea!
O, how marvelous Thy goodness,
Lavished all on me!
Yes, I rest in Thee, Beloved,
Know what wealth of grace is Thine,
Know Thy certainty of promise,
And have made it mine.

Simply trusting Thee, Lord Jesus,
I behold Thee as Thou art,
And Thy love, so pure, so changeless,
Satisfies my heart;
Satisfies its deepest longings,
Meets, supplies its ev'ry need,
Compasseth me round with blessings:
Thine is love indeed!

Bibliography

Concise Theology. Wheaton, Ill.: Tyndale, 1983.

"A Christian View of Man." In *The Christian Vision: Man in Society,* edited by Lynne Morris. Hillsdale, Mich.: Hillsdale College Press, 1984.

God's Words. Downers Grove, Ill.: InterVarsity Press, 1981.

Hot Tub Religion. Wheaton, Ill.: Tyndale House, Living Books, 1987.

Knowing God. Downers Grove, Ill.: InterVarsity Press, 1973.

"The Means of Growth." In *Tenth,* a periodical published by Tenth Presbyterian Church, Philadelphia.

Rediscovering Holiness. Ann Arbor, Mich.: Servant, Vine, 1992.

"Sacrifice and Satisfaction" and "To All Who Come." In *Our Savior God,* edited by J.M. Boice. Grand Rapids, Mich.:Baker, 1981.